Jack Connell

More Praise for *Portfolio Life*

"*Portfolio Life* is a timely book yet with a timeless message. As one who has benefited from Dave Corbett's common sense and sage advice, I heartily recommend this book to anyone interested in living a life that is enriching for oneself, family, friends, and community. It's a terrific tool to help make the choices needed to achieve prolonged satisfaction over a prolonged lifetime."

> — John D. Hamilton, Jr., former chairman of law firm Hale & Dorr (now WilmerHale)

"We are so conditioned to 'bop till you drop' that a life of rich balance, of giving, earning, striving, learning, and loving, is alien to many healthy and talented people. When by chance I read about New Directions when I was around 50, the idea of a 'life portfolio' struck a chord with me. I flew to Boston, became a client, and have been learning about possibility since then! *Portfolio Life* is a wonderful resource to tap this new paradigm."

> — Fred Reid, CEO, Virgin America

"*Portfolio Life* is on target in stressing lifelong learning and continual self-discovery. As our students know, these habits help people succeed in all aspects of life. This book offers an excellent way to invest in yourself."

> — Dipak C. Jain, dean, Northwestern University's Kellogg School of Management

"Most retirees don't plan how to use their time and end up worrying about where to have dinner or play golf. Women seem to handle change better than men, who tend to need more help preparing for post-career life. Given what 'non-retirees' could do for America, we're wasting a lot of talent. Dave Corbett shows us how to stop this."

> — Frank V. Cahouet, former chairman and CEO, Mellon Bank

"Most senior executives have small life portfolios when nearing retirement age. The life reinvention process should start much earlier and *Portfolio Life* is an excellent hands-on guide to take you there."

> — Windle B. Priem, former president and CEO,
>   Korn/Ferry International

"This book is important because there's little in professional and popular literature about the dynamic and dramatic changes that occur in the basic patterns of people's lives—changes they make by choice or as result of our 24/7 economy. The individual and historic examples Dave gives invite his readers to try out new possibilities in their own lives."

> — Marshall Carter, former chairman and CEO,
>   State Street Bank

"I think that *Portfolio Life* is a great idea and most helpful to those who want their later years to be fulfilling. I wish I had this book when I retired after 30 years as dean of the Washington Cathedral."

> — Francis Sayre, former dean,
>   Washington Cathedral, 30 years;
>   age 91; walks a mile a day

JB JOSSEY-BASS

PORTFOLIO LIFE

The New Path to Work, Purpose, and Passion After 50

David Corbett

with Richard Higgins

BICENTENNIAL

1807

WILEY

2007

BICENTENNIAL

John Wiley & Sons, Inc.

Published by Jossey-Bass
A Wiley Imprint
989 Market Street, San Francisco, CA 94103-1741   www.josseybass.com

Jossey-Bass books and products are available through most bookstores. To contact Jossey-Bass directly call our Customer Care Department within the U.S. at 800-956-7739, outside the U.S. at 317-572-3986, or fax 317-572-4002.

Jossey-Bass also publishes its books in a variety of electronic formats. Some content that appears in print may not be available in electronic books.

Library of Congress Cataloging-in-Publication Data

Corbett, David D.
    Portfolio life : the new path to work, purpose, and passion after 50 / David D. Corbett, with Richard Higgins.
       p. cm.
    Includes bibliographical references.
    ISBN-13: 978-0-7879-8356-7 (cloth)
    ISBN-10: 0-7879-8356-X (cloth)
    1. Life span, Productive. 2. Self-evaluation. 3. Post-retirement employment. 4. Success.
5. Retirement—Planning. I. Higgins, Richard. II. Title.
HB2583.C67 2007
332.024'014—dc22   2006019148

Printed in the United States of America
FIRST EDITION
HB Printing   10 9 8 7 6

CONTENTS

To all those who have a book stirring in them,
To all those who may have a book in them,
To all those who have a message they want to share,
Go for it!

FOREWORD

The pioneer feminist Betty Friedan often called the cultural constraints and limited options that confronted American women in the 1960s "the problem that had no name." Today, as the first of tens of millions of aging Baby Boomers reach their sixties and enter a new stage of life, one that could last for decades, they face what might be called an "opportunity with no name."

Neither old nor young, neither in midlife nor retired in any traditional sense, they face a crisis of identity that begins with a failure of words. Call them "senior citizens" or "elderly," for example, and they will refer you to their parents. The uncertainty they face extends to the very meaning of success. What, they must ask, might a person rightly aspire to during this space opening up in the lifespan?

Just as a problem that lacks a name is hard to solve, an opportunity without a name is hard to seize. We have not had a compelling vocabulary with which to capture the essence of this stage of contribution and renewal taking shape in front of our eyes. That has made it harder to convey the extraordinary opportunities now within reach of these Americans.

In *Portfolio Life*, David Corbett gives us more than a compelling new vocabulary. He transforms the old view of retirement—leisure time and family—into a new perspective that includes the familiar but adds the new: work, meaning, and purpose. Even better, he provides a step-by-step guide to get us there, a means of navigating both the inner terrain and questions of meaning as well as the outer questions of setting and accomplishing goals.

Friedan opened doors of opportunity for millions of women by pointing to the "problem that had no name." By focusing on the "opportunity with no name," Corbett may open similar doors for millions of people in the second half of life. When these gates have been flung open, people over 50 will rush through, thrilled to be in the thick of it, eager to dispel outdated notions of decline, and impatient to get started redefining their lives and changing the world.

It's only a matter of time.

MARC FREEDMAN

Marc Freedman is the founder and president of Civic Ventures, co-founder of the Experience Corps, and author of Prime Time: How Baby Boomers Will Revolutionize Retirement and Transform America *(PublicAffairs, 1999).*

PREFACE

For many years, I have worked with senior executives from corporations, professional services, education, and government in career transition. Often they would set their sights on "one more job" or career to set them up for a comfortable retirement—but had little to say about what might happen when that goal was met. People did not use to pay attention to their longevity track.

Now we do. The much-heralded gift of living longer in good health has opened up a whole new arena, a new adventure that could last for three or four decades after initial careers are done. Younger generations are also adding into the mix new ideas about work and how to balance it against other important things in life. We can learn from them.

This new stage of life is made more meaningful when people create a balance of work, learning, leisure, family time (ask me about my grandson), giving back, and whatever else has been simmering on the back burner of their hearts and souls during their careers. The balance can be tailored to one's personality and situation. I call this a *life portfolio,* because it holds an intentional combination of passions and pursuits. Those who do best at it step back early on, question whatever they may have learned about "retirement," envision new possibilities, and plan ahead.

That is my challenge to you. I want this book to encourage you to visualize such a life. I also want to provide practical help to readers who are willing to roll up their sleeves and get to work.

My own career in part reflects the emergence of this new viewpoint. I joined Johnson & Johnson (sales and marketing) after the Navy and business school in the 1960s and then moved into executive search to recruit senior people for client companies. In 1986, I founded New Directions to help executives and professionals leaving one job find the ideal next one. We still help clients land jobs, but more than ever we help them take a more holistic view of life goals. And interest in our Life Portfolio Program™ has grown dramatically. My own interest in portfolio as a path to personal happiness has also grown, in part because it allows me to give support and encouragement to others, something I have enjoyed doing as long as I can remember.

It is exciting to write a book about a territory of life so new that we are not quite sure what to call it. *Parade* magazine, in conjunction with the Harvard School of Public Health and the MetLife Foundation, asked readers this year to name this new stage or those in it. Almost four thousand suggestions poured in, including *rewirement, the third half,* and *prime time.* Readers gave *senior citizens* the Bronx cheer in favor of *seasoned citizens, legacy launchers,* and *OWLS* (for older, wiser, livelier souls). The number of entries practically equaled the number of letter writers, so there was no one winner. But the tone of views about this stage of life was decidedly upbeat.

The rise of this uncharted realm that is replacing retirement and the mind-set we need to enter it are the topics of this book. The opportunity this realm creates is not just for people of traditional retirement age. Careers, as traditionally defined, will become increasingly shorter in length than portfolios for many people. What is a *life portfolio?* It is a strategic plan of action but also an orientation to life, a perspective that spans today's goals and tomorrow's legacies. Because it can be woven into one's life as early as one's twenties, even as careers are pursued, and because it may last thirty or forty more years afterward, a portfolio is positioned to have more impact in shaping adulthood. Careers, in short, have a shelf life; portfolios can be timeless.

Writing this book has been on my mind for some time, so it is heartening to turn on the news and see that its relevance has only grown. One of my themes is that careers, even life portfolios, are not ends in themselves but should serve the larger goal of fulfilling our human potential, of embracing life with joy and a sense of purpose. My term for the resulting satisfaction is happiness, to which I devote the closing chapter. I have come to find that research on this topic, called *positive psychology,* is a major academic cottage industry. More than a hundred colleges and universities now offer classes about, in essence, what makes people happy. The one at Harvard University, with a staggering 855 students, even beat out Introductory Economics as the most popular course on campus this spring.

What is my definition of happiness? I am not certain, but the one offered by a former portfolio client is darn close. In his sixties, he resumed his love of flying. "Flying in the clouds for two hours and then seeing a clear runway at five hundred feet is happiness," he said. "It's almost spiritual."

Another theme I explore is the impact the longevity boom and the redefinition of aging is having on our sense of what we can accomplish in our lives. The U.S. Census Bureau's newest study of the aging population confirms a major increase in the number of years beyond age sixty-five in which older Americans can expect to be free of major disabilities. And at Oxford University, scientists reported that biomedical devices and anti-aging repairs may soon enable people to live regularly beyond 120 years, which used to be considered the outer limit of life. If you have not worked out a creative alternative to retirement, these extra years could lead to a very long game of canasta.

Medical science, in short, can slow the aging of your body, but only you can choose to keep your mind and spirit young. "When you have an extended life span without using extended consciousness," says Rabbi Zalman Schacter Shulomi, seventy-eight, a Jewish theologian, "you're dying longer, instead of living longer."

I call for new attitudes about our postcareer lives. One person who already has one is the older man who recently guided my wife, Linda, and me around a Maine history museum. When he told us he was retired, I asked him why he was leading tours. "The less you do," he said, "the older you get." Another person who reflects the new thinking is Marv Levy, who was recently hired to be general manager of the Buffalo Bills football team. Levy is eighty years old. "The age factor means nothing to me," he said after taking the job. "I'm old enough to know my limitations, and I'm young enough to exceed them."

I wrote this book to encourage people to think about what they want out of the *time bonus* we now get in later midlife. We cannot rely on corporations or social institutions to do this thinking for us. They are too slow to change. The evidence is the gap, which I explore in Chapter Seven, between the needs and realities of older

Americans and the very limited roles, options, and labels our society accords them. We can and should expect more employment
options, such as phased retirement, flexible schedules, sabbaticals,
and additional opportunities for employees to learn and grow. In
the long run, those changes are good for corporate America. But
ultimately, individuals must take the initiative.

The notion of portfolio is the centerpiece of the book. As a collection of personal holdings, including our unique gifts, values,
and passions, a portfolio represents who we are. It is about what
people are doing with their lives, how they're living, not their status
or wealth or how old or young they are. It even includes not doing,
if that means simply enjoying and reverencing life. This is still a
new way of thinking for people, perhaps including the reporter
who interviewed pop star Stevie Wonder. Why, the reporter wanted
to know, had Wonder waited ten years to produce a new album? "I
was just doing life," the singer replied with a smile.

Giving back to others is also central to portfolio. This returning to the world some of what we have been given can be done in
countless ways. It does not need to be a big gesture. You can give
in small ways, too, but do it constantly and consciously so that it
becomes a habit. In portfolio, we give back to the world some of the
immense gifts we have received.

An assessment is the prelude to portfolio. To know ourselves
better, we must slow down enough to feel our feelings and to hear
our deeper thoughts. We do this between the end of one life phase
and the beginning of another, a zone I call *neutral* (with a nod to
life-change specialist William Bridges [2004]). I like how one client
who needed to decompress described the process. After leaving a
job he had held for thirty years, he and his wife took a car trip with
no destination in mind. When they returned, I asked him where
they went.

"We just went to California and took a right," he said. "It was
great."

Ralph Waldo Emerson had a superb brief description of assessment: "The talent is the call." Whatever we do, he argued, we must
convert into an outlet for our identity. So it is really about having
the right attitude. Forget about what we think we *should* do, he
says. Our calling is that to which we bend easily, that which comes
naturally to us. All we have to do is pay attention. Assessment is

about finding clues to our real selves and knowing how to develop them.

The final chapters of *Portfolio Life* elaborate the disciplined, step-by-step process by which we enter into a life portfolio. One step is acquiring a new perspective on life, looking forward, not in the rearview mirror. Goals keep us on track and set expectations for our families, our support teams, and us. I explore long- and short-term portfolio planning in some detail, offering practical suggestions and exercises. I also examine some of the pockets of emotional turbulence people may encounter. A client recently told me something that suggests one of them. "As executives, our job is to solve problems at work," said the former chief operating officer. "When we are at home, we may try to solve problems there as well. That attitude doesn't work." Roles and relationships have to be rearranged.

I would be pleased if readers saw in this book the inspiring mind-set of Jonathan Livingston Seagull. Everyone remembers the storied seagull that refused to accept that flying was just a way to get food. Forget about flying for fun, the grown-up seagulls told him. What matters is not the flying but the eating. Young seagulls, they said, should bother only with the simplest facts of flight—how to get from shore to food and back again. Jonathan tried to obey, but he could not quell his urge to soar. And so he found the courage to learn to swoop and dive, and he found happiness in this. We can all learn from him. Don't abandon your dreams! And don't ever "retire" them!

Boston, Massachusetts   DAVID CORBETT
August 2006

PORTFOLIO LIFE

CHAPTER ONE

TRAILBLAZING

I work in a historic customshouse on Boston's waterfront. From my office, I see boats cut the harbor's currents and hear the snap of sails. A port is a transition point through which people and goods move. That makes it a good place for what I do, which is to help people navigate change by the compass of their life goals and set sail for new directions.

I founded my company, New Directions, in 1986, after years in the executive recruitment field. I wanted to try the other side of the fence—not helping companies obtain high-quality hires but helping talented individuals make career changes on their own terms. I realized that senior executives and professionals, in particular, needed to be bolder and more creative in embracing change and developing new opportunities, not merely settling for what is out there. There has not been a lot of tea or molasses passing through my building of late, but quite a few *people* have—the two thousand men and women who have come through our doors in order to chart a new course.

This work has given me an unusual vantage point on the emergence of a new life phase, which can extend anywhere from age fifty to age ninety. Americans are healthier and more vital during these years than we have ever been. More and more people are rejecting the idea of retirement as a permanent vacation and as they do resetting the once-fixed boundaries between career and retirement.

I want to share in this book the response we have created to meet this change, which I call a *life portfolio*. The central idea behind it is to step back and—using a step-by-step process—create

1

a balanced combination of five elements: (1) working in the form you want, (2) learning and self-development, (3) making time for personal pursuits and recreation, (4) enjoying family and friends, and (5) giving back to society. The combination of elements, or *portfolio,* is meant to reflect who you are and what you care about.

Whatever path you take during this new stage, the addition of fifteen to twenty-five years to late middle age is an extraordinary bonus. It can be a time of less stress, in which we can expand our minds and imaginations, play more, and enrich our wisdom. It can be a time of opportunity for us to give back some of what we have learned and gained. But it does not come with an owner's manual. In fact, most people are largely on their own as they enter it.

Throughout their careers, they received plenty of advice on how to save for retirement and what to do with their money. But in my view, they received too little advice, education, and training about how to rebalance their greatest assets: their time, their energy, and their gifts. In addition to having no clear guidelines, people who are age fifty and above were generally not taught as they grew up to think of this time as a period of personal growth. It's hardly surprising, then, that many of them feel off-kilter or in need of direction as they enter this new chapter in their lives.

Helping people in that situation move forward is one of two purposes I have in writing this book. With traditional retirement no longer a serious or viable postcareer option, I want to show readers how to build the creative alternative of a life portfolio, which rests on a balance of integrated elements. Drawing on years of experience, I will share the ideas behind it as well as strategies and practical steps that have proven to be effective.

What does the process look like? I believe that the first step in exploiting new possibilities is challenging your mind-set about the notion of "retirement." Take the time to investigate your assumptions or to "surface" any subconscious expectations about it. Talking with others is a good way to do this. Thoughts that you did not fully realize you had may tumble out. Be willing to learn and change your attitude. Why? Because how we think shapes our destiny. Our inward attitudes and assumptions contribute strongly to our outward reality. Also, be bold about reframing the potential vistas before you. We need to move beyond tinkering with retirement by adding more physical exercise or hiring retirees to work in retail chain stores, as welcome as those initial steps are. What I mean is that merely resolving to walk the course instead of taking the cart is not going to put you in a new frame of mind.

The second step is to revise the time line you have of your life. All of us need to plan for the likelihood that we may not fully retire until far later than we had ever imagined—or maybe never. Individuals vary, of course, but increasingly this means our eighties and nineties. I've been astonished by the number of people I have met or heard about who are working, active, and vital during those ninth and tenth decades of life. They are also the ones most likely to be perplexed by the word *retirement*.

This is all so relatively new that it still catches me off guard, and I bet it does so for you as well. Jeff Taylor is the founder of the Internet job site Monster.com. Recently, he started a new Internet-based company aimed at Web-surfing older Americans. A reporter asked him about his business plan. "I'm going to target the fifty- to hundred-year-old market," he said. Was this hyperbole? Possibly, but the mere fact that Taylor could speculate about the existence of such a consumer market and be taken seriously shows how much things have changed. We are in it for the long haul.

A third critical step is to recognize and embrace the larger personal opportunity or goal in this new stage of life. I have come to think that in order to have a successful postcareer life, one must grapple with an existential question: How do I go about discovering and experiencing what makes me happy, what gives me fulfillment and a sense of purpose? This means finding what creates, for each of us, the beginnings of a personal legacy. I believe that how well you live past age fifty depends in part on your rediscovering your unique gifts and purpose in life and then building a plan around developing them and executing that plan.

WIDER BENEFITS

My other main purpose in these pages is broader. For lack of forethought and creativity, our social institutions and corporate culture remain oriented—by default—toward a style of retirement in which people feel useless and adrift. Yet if we can adapt our thinking as a society to the new realities, there will be benefits for everyone. The "golden years" style of retirement was predicated on the assumption that aging equaled decline. Research has shown this assumption to be self-fulfilling. No wonder that half of full-time retirees say they are bored! I speak before groups of retired people. Listeners often approach me afterward to say how hard it has been to live without a purpose beyond lowering handicaps or monitoring the pool temperature.

Even with the recent shift to more active models, however, retirement in America remains a waste of what Marc Freedman, the founder and president of the nonprofit organization Civic Ventures, calls our nation's "enormous untapped resource"—the skills, experience, and wisdom of tens of millions of older Americans. This collective social capital is, to continue the metaphor, like a vein of gold in the ground that we refuse to mine and spend on good purposes.

Let's engage companies, universities, and public and religious institutions in generating new ways of thinking about the win-win opportunities that extended middle age affords. Let's make it more possible for those privileged enough to live a life portfolio to form partnerships with those who are not. Let's create excitement and curiosity around the idea that what follows a career is not retirement but a new perspective on life, characterized by experimentation, growth, giving back, and fulfillment.

One hurdle still to be overcome is what to call this new perspective, this stage that people in their fifties, sixties, seventies, and eighties are passing through. Most terms for it emphasize its relation to aging—*the third age, the second act,* and the many variations on retirement, including *unretirement, anti-retirement, revolving retirement, rewirement,* and *rehirement.* I call it *portfolio,* after the Life Portfolio Program™ we developed and launched at New Directions in 1994. A portfolio is, literally, a balanced collection of holdings related to one person, such as financial assets, job responsibilities, artistic works, and accomplishments. It's something portable, something you carry with you. The portfolio represents the whole. It represents what you have or have done as an expression of who you are. As work and life change, we take some elements out and put others in, which is just what we do when we reallocate or rebalance our investment portfolios.

It is true that, practically speaking, we may not take the portfolio approach or pursue a portfolio lifestyle until we have worked enough years or gained flexibility on the need to make money. But I also believe that there is a portfolio perspective or mind-set that we may enter into at any age. It's a lifelong way of looking at your career integrated into the rest of your life. Although I like *prime time* and sometimes use it, I feel that the term *portfolio* has advantages over the age- or stage-related terms. It speaks to what people are *doing* with their lives, how they are living, and what they value— not their age or stage of life. And portfolio, as I said, expands into a mind-set that is ageless, in the broader sense of figuring out what really matters in life.

FROM LIMBO TO LEGACY

The portfolio way of thinking about late middle age is still fairly new. For decades, Americans retired after sixty, with too many of them entering a period of inactivity. The hope of spending leisure time at the golf course, pool, or shopping mall was well marketed and widely shared, even if it masked a reality of boredom and depression. Not that retirees could go back if they wanted to. They would clean out the desk, go to the retirement party, and—upon leaving the office for the last time—hear a figurative loud click as if exiting a one-way door.

This approach has not completely faded. Senior-level executives and professionals still come to me after trying it. "I flunked retirement," one former CEO told me. I point out that in fact their vision of retirement "failed" them.

Yet there is a whole new life zone between career and complete retirement, one that seems to get wider every day. In this zone, new forms of paid and unpaid work, pursuits and possibilities, are becoming available. But it has been a do-it-yourself revolution to this point. Needed opportunities are not being created fast enough by companies or government programs. Progress *is* being made by those acting entrepreneurially between fifty and whenever who feel too young or energetic to retire yet who feel tired of work that no longer enriches their lives.

Older people who choose to pursue a second or third vocation are also increasingly physically able to do so. People may continue working at a reduced pace until age eighty-five and beyond. Their reasons are diverse. One is the need for income. Pension plans are no longer reliable, and Social Security benefits down the road are at risk. Investment portfolios took a hit after the dot-com bubble burst. The combination of much higher medical costs and longer life spans has made a long, fixed-income retirement prohibitively expensive for many people.

But there is also something else going on, which reflects a major theme of this book. It's a kind of revolt against the prospect of coasting through retirement. Many people in the zone between total career mode and total retirement want to discover or rediscover their passion. They would rather begin to create a legacy than to be in limbo. Even those who don't have to work to earn income want to work in order to turn careers into callings, success into significance.

They want to be active and contribute, start businesses, and be mentors and community leaders. They want to learn and create, paint and teach, earn black belts, write musicals, and invent better ways to do things. They are becoming entrepreneurs, going back to school, and using their experience to advise or create nonprofits and foundations. Instead of wanting to get ahead, they want to make a difference. Like good visionaries, they looked at the models handed to them—trudging along in golden chains or whiling away retirement in trivial pursuits—and decided they could do better.

I heard about a woman who captured this change eloquently not long ago. The speaker was Nancy Bailey Miller, a poet and teacher who helped run the chapel at Phillips Academy, in Andover, Massachusetts, where she delivered a sermon.

> At fifty-two, I still ask myself what I will be when I grow up. I have had many careers: middle school and high school English teacher, mother, Suzuki violin teacher, grant writer, poet, administrative worker in nonprofit, and now office manager here at Cochran Chapel. Does this mosaic comprise a sequence of jobs over thirty years or a "calling"? And now that our children are living away from home, which door is opening? Which threshold needs crossing? What am I supposed to be doing with my life? A job no longer defines who I am. Rather, who I am seems to be defining the jobs I do.

Jobs may have once defined who we were. Now, in the portfolio perspective, it's we who define the jobs we do. I believe that people

"Pruning" Oneself in Portfolio

There is no one right way to create a fulfilling alternative to retirement. Those who manage to do so, however, tend not to rush into a plan in order to fill a void. They slow down and take the time to assess their lives and their goals, during which they often look for ways to apply in a new way something they have done well in the past. The key is listening to themselves and to others and using intuition and instinct to identify what feels right. A former client who did just that and who agreed to share his story is Hank Schmelzer. Hank is the president of the Maine Community Foundation. How he got there is an example of how meaningful lives after fifty are created.

Hank began his work in philanthropy in 2000, at age fifty-seven and after thirty years in financial services. As the president and CEO of a Boston-based mutual fund company, he managed $8 billion and supervised 240 people. When he turned fifty, Hank set a goal of starting a new career in a different field within five years. When his fifty-fifth birthday came, he knew he had to try something different; he just didn't know what. At the time, the idea of walking away from his top-dog salary and perks, he told me, was "gut-wrenching." External events intervened. A corporate reorganization in 1998 gave him an opening: he took it and left. Hank became one of our clients at New Directions that year.

Hank took the time to decompress and conduct a thorough assessment before jumping on the next train at the station. William Bridges (2004), author of the book *Transitions,* calls this going into *neutral,* a term we frequently use at New Directions. Hank and his wife traveled to Italy, where for several months he skied every morning and studied Italian and wrote every afternoon. "Ideas kept coming to me," Hank told me. "For the first time, I was free to create. I loved skiing every day, studying Italian and writing every day. I began to clear away what felt insignificant." He later did a research project on government regulation of hedge funds through Harvard's Kennedy School of Government.

(Continued)

Hank said that as he sought his new path, he had to develop a deeper knowledge about what was most important to him, what fed his core self. We sometimes glibly call the assessment process "Me 101." On the surface, this sounds selfish. But in fact, people who truly know themselves tend to make life choices that give them the will and ability to help others. I believe deeply in serving others and changing our world for the better. Nevertheless, I tell this to clients who want to do just that: don't ask yourself what the world needs. Ask what makes you come alive and go do that, because what the world needs are people who have come alive.

I also advise clients in the assessment process to follow hints from their own histories. Hank did this and along the way found a great metaphor for career change. He had loved apple trees since growing up in a rural community outside Boston. His father had apple trees, and Hank worked in several orchards. So he decided to take a course on how to revitalize an apple tree.

"It was all about pruning the dead wood," he said, "about gradually getting rid of the weak branches and suckers and laterals that overlap each other. When you cut out the weak branches at the center of the tree, you make it a strong, healthy tree that holds the heavy fruit." Hank learned that an overcrowded apple tree is hard to protect from disease and produces small, dull apples. The older an apple tree grows, the heavier a pruning it needs.

"The teacher was this old Maine duffer named Amos. Someone asked how you know when you've pruned enough. Amos thought for a minute. Then he said, 'Well, stand back and look. If you think you can pick up your cat and toss him right through the middle, then you've pruned enough.'

"I loved that response, because it reminds me of what you have to do when you're going through career change. You have to try to open yourself up and get rid of all the dead aspects of yourself that weigh you down or drain the nutrients from your mind and soul. It's self-pruning, and it's what you have to do to rejuvenate and be able to grow productively."

In late 1999, a year after he had left his job, Hank heard about an opening at the Maine Community Foundation, which is based in Ellsworth, Maine, and which funds state projects in education, conservation and the environment, the arts, and social services. Hank said the job interested him for several reasons. He was trained as a lawyer, and through his years in the securities world, he had always remained interested in doing something connected to public service. In addition, he had resolved during self-assessment to seek a role that would tap into and build on his years of experience, and he discovered that the nonprofit world could benefit from his financial and managerial skills.

Plus he had Maine in his blood. His grandfather had been a minister in Maine. His mother had grown up there. And Hank had vacationed there as a child, graduated from the University of Maine, and now owned a second home there. "Every day after I learned about the job, it just got more and more interesting and engaging," he said.

Hank took the job in 2000. The change took some adjusting, he recalls, because the nonprofit world, which prizes consensus, is a different animal from the hard-driving corporate culture he came from. "I knew my skills were valued, but it took awhile for people to accept me and for me to feel comfortable in that culture." But it worked. Since he took over, the endowment of the Maine Community Foundation has more than doubled, from $78 million to $180 million, permitting it to make more grants and help more people. Today he calls his new job "just about perfect" for him. The knot he used to have in his gut Sunday nights, thinking about the coming week, has vanished, and he says he loves getting up each day and going to work. "We're trying to make life better," he explains. And he gets an occasional bonus that he truly values: Hank has traded his Blackberry pager for visits in his jeep on bumpy back roads to blueberry farmers in Maine.

who do this during extended middle age have come to recognize and accept that their chance to be happy, to be fully who they are meant to be on this earth, is now. This comes at different times to each of us. Sadly, some never realize it. I urge those just awakening to this feeling to persevere. Keep this fire burning, and as you plan for the future, don't let the concept of passive retirement even creep into your thinking. You may not do all you hope, but cultivating the ability to imagine the possibilities in front of you is the first step.

RECLAIMING OURSELVES

I mentioned earlier that building New Directions has been a great vantage point from which to observe the emergence of this new perspective on later life. I'd like to tell you some of the broad lessons I have learned to set a context for my discussion of portfolio. One is how many clients have been willing to help others, even as they seek help planning their own careers and lives. Years ago, I started a foundation to put the managerial skills and experience of our clients to work helping low-income people find employment. So far, some 450-plus clients have volunteered as job mentors. Many of them may not have known it inside, but they were simply waiting to be asked. A surprise lesson has been how often our alumni, as we call them, have compared their time of transition with us with going back to school to get recharged—except that, in this case, they "majored" in their own lives.

I have also learned that senior executives who are able to revitalize a company, shift its strategic focus, or adapt its offerings may not be able to do that for themselves. We have had clients who could manage huge, multinational corporations but hit stumbling blocks managing their own lives.

The most striking surprise, however, has been how much the process of career change entails a more subjective, interior, and even spiritual process: nothing less than the rediscovery and reclaiming of our unique spark as individuals. When people lose or surrender a job, they have to learn to stop identifying themselves by their title, company, or industry. They have to discover or rediscover the deeper identity, which probably should have been their ground, their foundation, all the way along.

I've found that a wide-ranging and serious process of assessment can enable them to revise and deepen their understanding of the specific skills, areas of insight, motivations, or experiential wisdom that each of us has to offer—as well as how to hone them for new uses. It means coming to know our individual distinctive gifts, the "light" within ourselves that we should never hide.

Not everyone can do this. There are many emotional obstacles, which I will address. But for those who can, the rewards are manifold. At New Directions, we take as our mission statement a remarkable thought from the philosopher Martin Buber:

> Every person born in this world represents something new, something that never existed before, something original and unique and every man's foremost task is the actualization of his unique, unprecedented and never-recurring possibilities [1960, pp. 12–13].

I truly believe Buber when he says that everybody has something unique to offer. It's become my mission and my privilege to help people get in touch with it, to identify the work or activity that capitalizes on and leverages their assets and skills. The life window of portfolio time is our chance to *actualize* these gifts.

Of course, no one likes to surrender familiar ways of thinking or doing in order to reinvent him or herself. Psychologist Erich Fromm called the process that Buber describes as "giving birth" to oneself, but he also observes that some people never do it. "We should be fully born when we die," he wrote. But too many people, he added, "die before they are born."

For all the difficulty, however, this is a good news story. That good news is that we have the gift of these extra years and that they are full of possibilities. To seize them, you have to become an entrepreneur of your own life. *Develop them.* People who think like that do better as they go from careers to life portfolios. They figure things out, not *by* themselves necessarily, but *for* themselves. Disappointments, rejections, losses—all are opportunities. No does not mean never. Everything is negotiable. They ask, "What if?" They are looking for better ways. They make choices. Maybe they are wrong at first, but they jump in. They become players, not spectators, in the game of life.

If you can direct that kind of curiosity *inward*, you will discover the values, interests, and abilities at your core, at the nut and fiber of who you are. Those qualities, once identified, can be applied to opportunities and communicated to others in ways as exciting as the business plan of any start-up.

I sometimes struggle with this because it may sound selfish. But if this kind of self-actualization makes us stronger and thus more able to give back to others, and I believe that it does, then why shouldn't we speak of it with boldness and conviction? It's usually people in touch with their passions who are on the front lines of volunteering. "If you want to lift yourself up," said Booker T. Washington, "lift up someone else." It's just as true that if you lift up yourself, you are more likely to lift up someone else.

So dream anything, even if it seems frivolous. "Those who dream by day," Edgar Allan Poe wrote in his short story "Eleonora" in 1842, see things that "escape those who dream only by night." Challenge tradition. Look at the transition to extended middle age as not another career change, but a life change. If you are fifty-five, it could be thirty years or longer before you are ready to stop work completely.

My message is not just for those in extended middle age. To those who are younger, perhaps still building a career, I say to you, *plan for it!* No one should be caught flat-footed by the lengthening of middle age. Life portfolios don't appear full bloomed out of thin air after decades spent relentlessly focused on careers. Ideally, they are woven continually in the back of our minds throughout our careers, during the valleys but also the peaks. Approached in this spirit, portfolio becomes an ongoing, ageless framework for self-renewal.

If you are younger, don't let the recent gains in longevity provide an excuse to delay thinking about what you will do. It's human nature for people to say that aging begins from ten to twenty years *later* than their current age. It actually starts on a physical and mental level before we know it, with changes in cognitive function and flexibility perceptible in one's late thirties and forties, according to Joseph Coughlin, the founder and director of the Massachusetts Institute of Technology's AgeLab. "Aging comes sooner than we'd like," he says. Moreover, the warp speed at which knowledge and technology are moving, he adds, puts everyone, including people under age forty, at risk of not adapting to new realities quickly enough. I know Joe because I sit on the advisory board of the AgeLab. One of its basic messages is that aging is becoming less a chronological state and more a state of mind.

This leads me to some advice that you probably would not hear at MIT but which has served me well: it wasn't raining when Noah built the ark. Plan! Anticipate. Do the homework. Assess and reassess your assets, skills, gifts, and goals all along the way. Know your own callings, energies, and passions. Extend your support networks or create new ones, and make doing these things your agenda day after day after day, even if it competes with another full-time job before prime time sets in. That is a risk that must be taken.

If the beginnings of plans are made and the seeds of future activities are sown in advance, then when change comes, we don't have to go back to square one, asking ourselves, what am I going to do? A new pursuit in line with your true self will be at least a little closer; the networks we need to generate new opportunities will be more advanced. For people in the midst of their careers, this requires maintaining a sense of life goals on a track above corporate or job goals. That might have sounded self-serving not long ago, but today it's a realistic response to the immense change in the modern workplace. So develop the habit of introspection and the entrepreneurial mind-set described in this book. You'll need them when your career is no longer the centerpiece of your life.

CHAPTER TWO

A NEW BEGINNING

I met recently on Boston's Long Wharf with an impressive group of people. In the room were about a dozen senior lawyers from a traditional firm, individuals who were highly skilled at mastering new situations. But when the topic of career timetables and leadership succession at their firm arose, the sense of foreboding was palpable. They shifted uncomfortably in their seats. In voices less resonant or certain than before, several lawyers said that they had not gotten around to planning for their lives after the firm. These men and women seemed to know only what they did *not* want to happen rather than what they *did* want to happen, and this made them anxious.

Their anxiety was understandable. There are few clear expectations now of what one does between the ages of fifty and eighty, how one does it, and how to tell if one has succeeded at doing it. This lack of concrete measures can be unsettling. For many, prior expectations they had have been upended.

As it happens, most of the lawyers I talked with that day were closing in on or had turned sixty years old. During 2006, 3.3 million Americans will reach that age. When they were young—make that young*er*—turning sixty was taken as a yellow caution signal: get ready to step down in about five years, to become a "retiree."

Yet as people turn sixty today, the hit-the-brakes message is missing. The prospect of prolonged good health for years to come has created a new spectrum of opportunities between midlife and the onset of true old age. Most people no longer retire for good at age sixty-five. Two out of three Americans work for pay, full-time or part-time, after reaching that age. In survey after survey, four of five people indicate that they intend to work.

Retirement as a complete cessation of work and withdrawal from society is fast becoming history. Why? There is no shortage of practical reasons, as we will see in the next chapter. Here I want to explore my belief that people are *choosing* to weave work into their life portfolio and are doing so because of a basic psychological change in how we see later life. What used to be passage suffused with memories has become a portal to new beginnings.

THE RISE AND FALL OF RETIREMENT

Let's begin by looking at the role of work in this interior shift. Satisfying work that permits you to be at your best is a source of meaning and connection. It may be the key to a middle path between a full-bore career—and fully boring leisure. For most of us, doing work that we both enjoy and do well is a way to remain connected and engaged and to make a contribution to others. That is why so many people are determined to continue using their experience, skills, and energy.

What is happening is that we are moving back closer to the historical norm in which people worked, remained active in society, and kept a hand in things as long as they were physically able. This pattern held for centuries. When America was an agrarian society, retirement was largely unknown. If people didn't die with their boots on, they died not long after they unlaced them. And this was not the case only for farmers or merchants who had no one to take over their work or no economic choice. Older people of means worked to feel productive and to stay connected with their society. Work expressed who they were.

John Quincy Adams, the sixth president (and son of the second), is a case in point. After leaving the White House, Adams at sixty-three became a freshman U.S. congressman and served with distinction until he was eighty years old. It was his tireless work as a legislator, not his presidency, that sealed his legacy. Adams explained his decision in terms that hint at what gerontologists are only now coming to understand. "The mind of an old man is like an old horse," Adams said at age ninety. "If you would get any work out of it, you must work it all the time."

The spread of industrialization created a need to change this pattern. To ramp up productivity, factories and mills wanted to replace older workers with younger ones. Retirement was born. A private railroad created America's first industrial pension plan in 1874. It set the age of eligibility at sixty-five, reasoning that after that point workers were too old to run a train. (Today we would say this is no way to run a railroad!) In 1934, a federal law creating a pension fund for American railway workers adopted sixty-five as its eligibility age. The next year, when the historic Social Security Act was passed, it adopted and institutionalized that retirement age.

With this new notion came a change in social attitudes toward aging. Josiah Quincy, a president of Harvard College, reflected the old view. In 1850, when he turned seventy-four, he *began* to keep a daily journal and vowed that he would stay busy, being determined to avoid the "indifference to labor" that was one of the "dangers of old men." A half century later, however, the tune had changed. In a controversial speech at Johns Hopkins University, Dr. William Osler, a pioneer of modern medicine, decried the "uselessness of men" above age sixty and cited the "incalculable benefit" to society if they stopped working.

After 1935, the promise of federal benefits, the growth of private pension plans, and the imposition of mandatory retirement all contributed to making retirement a seemingly permanent fixture in American life. People began to retire completely at earlier and earlier ages—a secular trend that would continue for fifty years.

By the 1950s, the developer Del Webb saw a bonanza in selling retirement housing as the reward one deserved in life's "golden years." On January 1, 1960, he opened Sun City near Phoenix, the first real estate development in America that required buyers to be of a certain age. The hugely successful retirement community, which has had many sequels, came to define and popularize the old model of retirement.

Webb did package Sun City as a place for "active retirement" and "an active new way of life." But in practice, the available options were little more than the community pool, the community golf course, or canasta. Over time, the golden-years style of retirement became associated, literally and metaphorically, with a long leisurely cruise. The mentality was to leave work as soon as possible and do as little as possible for as long as possible. You paid your dues; now it was time to sit back and collect. This proved enervating for many people. They had looked forward to retirement but were miserable puttering about in golf carts and watching too much television. One study in the 1990s found that retired Americans were watching forty hours of television per week, which is as long as a regular workweek but far less interesting. Many have told me that lacking goals made them uneasy.

In the 1990s, Americans began to reject this scenario. The trend toward retiring earlier that had begun in the 1930s peaked and reversed. Workers at age sixty-five began to remain in the paid workforce or—if they had already retired—to return to it. Today some older workers stay in the same job but work for fewer hours or shoulder fewer responsibilities. Others may choose new full- or part-time jobs that suit their interests and financial needs. Or they may cycle in and out of work, creating a subcategory of *revolving retirement*. Labor economists say that one out of three new jobs in the United States is being scooped up by people over sixty.

Increasingly, people work until very late in life, as if following William Safire's advice in his last regular syndicated opinion column: "Never Retire!" As his source, Safire cited his friend and pioneering geneticist James Watson, who helped discover the structure of DNA. But of course, many great minds have had this thought, as a history buff like Safire would be the first to attest. Asked if he planned to retire, Winston Churchill shot back, "Not until I am a great deal worse and the Empire a great deal better."

The social meaning of retirement is changing as well. It was not very long ago that retirement was a sign of status, and the more leisure in your life the more status you had. Retiring early was admired. In the early 1990s, a man who cashed in his chips at age forty-nine and could afford to do nothing was seen as pretty darn successful. Not any longer. Status now goes to the older adult who continues to work.

Baby Boomers typically get credit for the reinvention of retirement, but the data show that retirement choices had begun to change significantly before the oldest boomers (born in 1946) turned fifty in 1996. So perhaps the real trailblazing credit goes to the so-called pre-boomer generation, those born from 1935 through 1945, although it is true that boomers have magnified the rate of change since then. And the golden-years dream did not succumb only to boomer preferences. It made no sense in light of longer life spans, the uncertain future of Social Security, a decline in fixed-benefit pension plans, and skyrocketing health care costs.

The final coup may have been the stock market meltdown of 2000, which brought many a retirement finance fantasy down to earth.

What is going on in America, by the way, is part of a global phenomenon. In 2004, Age Wave, a market research and consulting firm, conducted a global study of attitudes about retirement for HSBC, a global bank. Age Wave surveyed eleven thousand adults in ten different countries. It found three-quarters rejected mandatory retirement and supported the view that people should be allowed to work as long as they want.

A NEW VISION OF LIFE

Why is this occurring? Why is not just the style but also the idea behind retirement in such upheaval?

Rather than merely extending the end of life, the added years from recent gains in longevity are perceived as lengthening later midlife, that hard-to-quantify transition stage after careers and families are built and stable. Many seventy-year-olds today are as mentally and physically fit as fifty-year-olds were not long ago. A report by World Health Organization estimates that children born today in the United States, once they live to age fifty, have a fifty-fifty chance of living to be to a hundred years old. Scientists foresee the average life expectancy of American women reaching a hundred by 2070.

The psychological impact of this has been profound. People are revising their assumptions—not only about the lengths and shapes of careers but also about what they can do in their lifetime. I like how Freedman, the Civic Ventures president, puts it. The old dream of freedom *from* work, he says, has been replaced by the freedom *to* work in rewarding jobs in new fields. In the same way, people used to retire *from* something, such as a company, a job, a career. Now they retire *to* something positive.

People are working later into life to build routine mental stimulation into their lives. Work can provide deeper social bonds than those formed in casual socializing. It provides structure. For many people, meaningful work is how they create value. It's critical to how they see themselves, so they continue to work because that is who they are. Screen legend Bette Davis, who took acting roles into her late eighties, described that belief colorfully. "I will not retire," she said, "while I've still got my legs and my makeup box."

"The break is set for eleven. Pass it on."

A Most Tiring Word

The first recorded use of the word *retire* described a military retreat in 1533, and retirement has been stopping advances ever since. The English verb *to retire* combines *re-* (back) and *tirer,* an old French verb meaning to draw or pull. Before the advent of old-age benefits in the early twentieth century began to shift its common use, to retire was chiefly to *withdraw* from action, *disengage, recede, detach, pull back, enter seclusion.* We "retire" to bed, to conk out. It also meant being alone. Henry David Thoreau liked to hike in "splendid retirement."

As a verb, retire is passive. It can't stand on its own two syllables. We don't retire; we retire *from* or *to* something. In fact, the whole concept is defined by what we don't do (work), not what we do! Retirement conveys or implies decline, inactivity, or

(Continued)

separation from one's source of power or status. It gives us that shrinking feeling, as another nineteenth-century writer illustrated when he wrote that in old age a person's spirit seems to "contract its domain, *retiring* within narrower walls by the loss of memory."

When someone says to us, "I'm retiring," we usually give a thumbs-up reply and offer congratulations. But doesn't the remark also trigger some other subconscious thoughts? Our friend is about to *turn in his badge, hang up his spurs,* or *head out to pasture.* Others have not minced words. "Retirement," said Ernest Hemingway, "is the ugliest word in the English language." The great cellist Pablo Casals didn't pull strings: "To retire is to die," he said. And French philosopher Simone de Beauvoir said that it's like being thrown on a "scrap-heap."

Retirement is a downer. It makes people go downhill. How do I know? Just look at this list of definitions and synonyms culled from various sources.

Retire
go
hide
pass
leave
demit
recede
evanesce
withdraw
go to bed
step down
melt away
go offstage
wash hands of
head to pasture
turn in one's badge
hang up one's spurs
disappear from sight
seek a quiet life (as a hermit)
give up an office or occupation
shrink from society or publicity

Today, retirement is getting a public image makeover that any celebrity would die for. People are trying to adapt it to the social reality of postcareer life in America today. Articles, books, and think tank reports speak of *unretirement, nonretirement, anti-retirement, semi-retirement,* and *serial, revolving,* and *phased* retirement. More imaginatively, or perhaps just using more linguistic Botox, people have coined such terms as *rehirement, refirement, protirement,* and *re-aspirement.*

This semantic salvage job is a waste of time. Why don't we just hang up this word's letters, take off its badge, and put it out to pasture? Our minds are always drawn back to messages that contradict—and undersell—the exciting opportunities for engagement before older Americans today.

Continuing to work past retirement age can also be a way to enlarge our lives and find new purposes, a reason to get up in the morning. A recent survey by Civic Ventures found that half of adults between age fifty and seventy say they would like to find work that enhances the well-being of others, in particular in education and social services. In the portfolio clients I work with, I see a genuine desire for work that enriches them beyond paying the bills.

Earlier I mentioned John Quincy Adams as someone who lived a vital and engaging life in his later years. Today we have, among others, Jimmy Carter, who will also be remembered for what he accomplished in his "presidential retirement"—bridging differences in conflicts, advancing peace, serving others, and even striving to change attitudes about aging.

To me, this is the heart of the change. Americans are coming to realize that the second half of life can mean a second wind. We have come to realize that we are not done at sixty, not at seventy, not at eighty, and maybe not at ninety. Fewer people see their arrival into these years as a time to sit back, heave a sigh, and collect their dues from the world. It's now a time to step up, contribute, and serve, a time to learn and try new things. There is much behind, but there is more ahead.

People increasingly see the close of their primary careers not only as an ending but also as a new beginning, a chance to set new goals and start new activities. It has become an adventure rather than a process to be dreaded. The language of retirement was always in the past tense. It was a time to look back over our lives. Now it's a beginning. It's a time to look forward to new expeditions across our interior landscapes.

Not surprisingly, those looking forward in this way want to work on their own terms and for their own reasons. I have seen marketing execs turn to oyster farming, bankers start teaching high school, and lawyers take up the study of bird migration. Many clients bring their managerial skills to nonprofit organizations or write books. One client in our Life Portfolio Program is finishing a book on the history of olive oil. Some seek to use their experience to benefit the public good by serving as mentors, community leaders, and government consultants. Others turn their hobbies or creative potential into income-producing businesses.

These are still somewhat novel paths, but the longevity boom is slowly changing attitudes about the options open to older Americans. Over time, this will make creative alternatives to retirement more available and easier to plan and implement.

Although work is a key indicator of changing attitudes about our prime time years, it's only one element in a balanced life portfolio. Play and recreation, creativity and joyfulness, are important and must be given free reign. This new vision of life after fifty includes time to renew, repair, or just enjoy our personal relationships. At New Directions, the clients who do best are those who stay connected and build relationships with others. Ongoing learning to stimulate our minds and spiritual growth to cultivate wisdom also are key ingredients. Another major area of focus is engaging in humanitarian or community-based work as a way of giving back to society some of the riches we have been blessed with.

People find that the portfolio approach allows them to create a better balance or mix of those elements. I've worked with many business executives who have had to deal with corporate downsizing, layoffs, and mergers that left them feeling they had no control over their lives. Some worked in corporate or professional cultures that lured them into a kind of absentee life. Richly rewarded in salary, they owned beautiful homes but were too busy to enjoy them and ended up delegating the "mundane" personal tasks of daily life, including care of their children, to a cadre of paid agents. Now they want to take back control of their lives and strike a better balance.

One challenge people face as they make this transition is dealing with a perceived loss of identity. The absence of reassuring routines and relationships can contribute to a sense of being disoriented, which may hinder us. I work sometimes with college administrators and faculty. A professor told me that he had delayed accepting retirement for years because he felt it would show he was no longer the scholar and person he had always been and continued to be. At seventy, he phased back to half-time teaching but had to surrender his full faculty status. "I don't identify as a retired person," he said. "It's the symbolism that made me reluctant to retire and still makes me uncomfortable."

A publishing firm manager came to us at age sixty-three to help her leave her job. A few months after seeking help planning her transition, she withdrew from the process and eventually from contact with us. A year and a half later, she called and said she needed to resume the aborted process. I asked why she had not been ready earlier. "What scares me most is that I'll be dismissed, that I won't be thought of as useful anymore."

The word *dismissed* turns up in many client stories as they relate fears of or feelings about being unwanted, not sought out for counsel. They feel that they will not count anymore. Almost all of them know on a deeper level that measuring their self-worth by the size of their in-box is not constructive, but the fear is deep and to a degree normal. I tell them that one way to get over their hump is to put energy into their relationships, sharing, giving, and reaching out to others.

Leave No Graybeard Behind!

Despite the changes I have been describing, many business folk are ill prepared to make the most of their portfolio time. Given how fast things have changed, this does not surprise. Fred Astaire was right. To make a success of aging, you have to start young. Unfortunately, most of us don't. "For most of my working life, my goals were my company's goals," a fifty-eight-year-old CEO told me recently. "I didn't take time for my own goals. I'm realizing that I should have started planning for this time much sooner."

I meet many fully retired people who say to me, "I've never been busier." Often I feel that is a cover. Judging from what they tell me, they are too busy with activities that don't cut to the quick of their lives and too lacking in the kind of goals that sustain us. Meeting them redoubles my motivation to get people active and engaged again.

The new mind-set can also be unsettling to people who are bone weary from a lifetime of work and want only to rest. Of course, we all need and want this. Rest makes labor bearable. But the flip side is also true: work, along with the sense of purpose that comes from fulfilling work, makes rest enjoyable and tolerable. A friend used to love golf when he had a demanding job that he needed to get away from. Then he retired, played every day, and became bored out of his mind. "It used to be like skipping school, but now it's no fun," he told me. "I guess I need a job to escape from."

The portfolio model is predicated on balance, so it is physically and mentally restorative. To keep it that way, people adjust their level and type of work to their changing needs (including age, interests, opportunities, finances). In my book, that makes it more restful than an endless cruise ship voyage from which we never return. I don't think we should be sorry to see the vacation model of retirement go.

Chapter Three

New Realities

It would be great if this new vision of life were simply a triumph of the human spirit. It is, to be sure, but we are also getting a good shove from many external social and economic factors. In the last chapter, I addressed how internal psychological attitudes and assumptions about retirement are changing and the cultural implications of this change. In this chapter, I will lay out some of the external social, demographic, economic, and workplace trends that are influencing the options people have and the choices they will make in planning alternatives to retirement.

These trends are based on a mix of hard data and more subjective evidence. Some, such as increasing life expectancy, or the projected demand for the skills and experience of older workers in the next two decades, are easily demonstrated. Others, such as the premium that people are placing on personal time, are harder to quantify but no less real. There is no question, however, that together these new realities are powerful drivers of what I call the *portfolio mind-set*.

Bonus Years

The most powerful driver is the dramatic change in longevity. The reality is that people are no longer old at age sixty-five. In 1962, *Time* magazine ran a cover story about the aging of America—pointing out that between 1920 and 1960 the number of people age seventy-five and up more than doubled. Since then, longevity has continued to grow, as fitness among older people has increased and death rates from cancer and heart disease have gone down. One in eight Americans is now at least age sixty-five. Yet when the Social Security Act was passed in 1935, only one in twenty qualified for the new program. And the trend will continue. The number of Americans over sixty-five is expected to grow from 35 million in 2000 to 71.5 million in 2030, at which time one in five Americans will be over sixty-five. It has even been estimated that half of all people ever born in the United States who lived to age sixty-five are alive today (and I hope they all buy a copy of this book!). Biologists say that new technologies to replace parts or reverse aging in the human body could soon have people in industrialized countries living to age one hundred. At a recent scientific forum, Aubrey de Grey, a biomedical gerontologist at Cambridge University in England, predicted a 50 percent chance during the next twenty years of "creating therapies to give middle-aged people an extra twenty-five years of life."

The trend has begun to alter public attitudes about aging and the stages of the life cycle. Let's say that during most of the last century, adults were "young" during their twenties, entered middle age at thirty, and became "old" at sixty. In the re-scaled life cycle, young adulthood continues to the mid-thirties. Early middle age occurs from thirty-five to fifty, and late or extended middle age is from fifty to sixty-five. The period from sixty-five to eighty—and here we get into the unnamed portions of the age map—is the gray zone of what has been called the *young old* stage. Because people in this group are still vital, this stage is closer in spirit and identity to late middle age than to true old age, which may not begin until age eighty-five.

The revised view, then, creates about a twenty-year gap between our former and current concepts of old age. That is a fabulous gift of time in which to grow, enjoy life, and try to make the world, or at a minimum your world, a better place. Conversely, if you retire at age sixty and live to eighty-five, that is a very long time to just sit around.

Abraham Lincoln noted that what counts is not the number of years in your life but "the life that is in your years." It might please him to know that his countrymen are not only living longer, they are healthier and more vital in their extra years. Studies show a marked decline over the last twenty years in chronic disabilities among people over age sixty-five. This improvement in health is due to advances in medical treatments and the increased attention

Americans pay to diet and exercise. Older Americans are fitter than ever, and maintaining fitness over fifty is a growth industry. According to United States Masters Swimming, Inc., nine hundred of its forty thousand members are age seventy-five and up. At its meets, the group divides its older competitive swimmers into five age groups: seventy-five to seventy-nine, eighty to eighty four, eighty-five to eighty-nine, ninety to ninety-four, and ninety-five to ninety-nine! One in eight of USA Triathlon's fifty thousand members is over age fifty. These are people who have caught on to the discovery, one backed by scientific research, of the new paradigm of aging. Gerontologists now believe that physical and mental health in later life are far more likely to be attributable to personal choices concerning diet, exercise, and self-care practices than to our genetic makeup (Figure 3.1).

How does a longer life span affect retirement? It removes two core assumptions that created the concept. One was that older workers were not as strong or as quick as younger ones, which in physical labor affects productivity. Retirement was in part a way to replace older workers with younger ones. Today, however, only one in ten jobs in the United States is physically demanding. Regardless, health advances have made older workers more vigorous.

The other assumption concerned the length of retirement. At the outset, Social Security payments were conceived as an end-of-life

FIGURE 3.1. PROJECTED OLDER POPULATION (1940–2050).

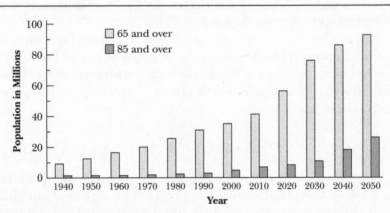

Source: U.S. Census Bureau.

benefit that would last for a short time. But in the past century, Americans' average life expectancy from birth has grown by thirty years, from forty-eight to seventy-eight years. From 1900 to 2000, the average length of retirement grew from one to nineteen years. Longevity accounted for much of this, but so did the fact that from 1935 to 2000 there was a trend toward retiring earlier and earlier.

Recently, however, the Bureau of Labor Statistics caught on to the fact that the group it designates *early retirees* are not in fact quitting work for good and so are not "retiring." These people may use their Social Security benefits to offset the loss of a job or for other reasons, but a growing percentage of those who tap into their retirement benefits early seek new employment. (That would make sense; labor economists estimate that one of every four new jobs in America goes to people age sixty and up.) In a 2004 Merrill Lynch study, only 17 percent of the more than three thousand boomer respondents said they plan to stop working for pay, and 42 percent said they hope to transition between work and leisure throughout life. And not everyone seeking new opportunities does so for just financial reasons.

The size of the Boom generation—some 78.2 million Americans who were born between 1946 and 1964 were alive in 2005—will amplify the cultural impact of the longevity boom (Figure 3.2). This year, more than half of this cohort is at least fifty years old, with a new one crossing into that age zone every seven seconds. (However with boomers, even numerical age is relative. Studies show that most boomers see themselves as ten to twenty years younger than they actually are.)

Those who have been watching know that this generation has used its demographic heft to reshape many sectors of American life—housing, education, work, politics, consumerism, and spirituality, to name a few. Now it will put its own stamp on the postcareer phase of life.

RETIREMENT ECONOMIC FORECAST: CLOUDY

The second major force unraveling the concept of retirement is economic. Recent economic shifts raise real warning flags about giving up on making money too early in life, but they are not definitive drivers in the reinvention of retirement. Despite the dire warnings

FIGURE 3.2. BOOMERS BY THE NUMBERS.

- **78.2 million:** number of baby boomers in the nation in 2005
- **3 out of 4:** ratio of boomers who say they expect to work past 65
- **every 7 seconds:** how often someone in the United States turns age 50
- **7,918:** average number of Americans who turn each day 60 this year
- **20 percent:** segment of population projected to be age 66 to 84 in 2030.
- **51 percent:** share of boomers who are women
- **81.6:** average life expectancy of people 60 years old today
- **1st (names):** James and Mary led the lists in 1946. Today, James ranks 17 for boys, Mary, 63 for girls.
- **$2 trillion:** estimated annual spending power of all boomers
- **$45,000:** average boomer annual household spending. Those age 45 to 54 have the highest average income ($68,028) and spending ($50,101)
- **60 percent:** projected ratio of men age 60 to 64 in the workforce in 2012, versus 54 percent in 1992
- **2 to 1:** the projected ratio of workers to Social Security beneficiaries in 2031; (the ratio is now 3.3 to 1)

Sources:

AARP
Helping Aging Boomers to Age in Place
www.aarp.org/about_aarp/aarp_leadership/on_issues

The Boomer Project
www.boomerproject.com/resources.html

Bureau of Labor Statistics
www.bls.gov/cex/2003/Standard/age.pdf

Centers for Disease Control and Prevention
National Vital Statistics Reports
www.cdc.gov/nchs/data/nvsr/nvsr51/nvsr51_03.pdf
www.cdc.gov/nchs/data/vsus/vsus_1946_1.pdf

Congressional Budget Office
September 2004 labor force projections,
www.cbo.gov/ftpdocs/58xx/doc5803/09-15-LaborForce.pdf

Del Webb 2004 Baby Boomer Survey
Statistics on Empty Nests and Retirement
http://www.escapehomes.com/main.aspx?tabid=45&itemid=186

(Continued)

FIGURE 3.2. CONTINUED.

Merrill Lynch
New Retirement Survey
www.ml.com/?id=7695_7696_8149_46028_46503_46635

Metlife Mature Market Institute
Demographic Profile of American Baby Boomers
www.metlife.com/WPSAssets/13321348111123273772V1FBoomer
ProfileRel.pdf

U.S. Census Bureau Data on Aging
Facts for Features or Special Editions
www.census.gov/population/pop-profile/dynamic/AgeSex.pdf

about the admittedly low rate of retirement savings in America, the massive debt the Baby Boom generation has accumulated, and the perilous state of Society Security entitlements, Americans in extended middle age have amassed more wealth than any previous generation. According to the Federal Reserve, average net worth of families headed by fifty-five- to sixty-four-year-olds is growing faster than any other type of family. Baby Boomers are estimated to control $7 trillion in financial assets, more than two-thirds of American capital. You could call that the good news. The bad news is that there are four good reasons why complete retirement from income-producing work is less viable during this new stage of life:

• The costs of Social Security entitlements are rising and will rise more because of the Baby Boom generation. In 2000, those benefits consumed the equivalent of 4.6 percent of the Gross National Product. By 2050, that figure would rise to 7.4 percent under the present system. Clearly, the retirement age will have to be raised or benefits cut or both. (As an optimist, I would like to say that things are not as bad as the satirical newspaper *The Onion* wrote last year. In a parody story, it claimed that certain politicians, in a bid to "save" Social Security, favored allowing people to bet their retirement savings on their favorite sports teams!)

• Fewer people have a defined benefit pension, which pays out at the same rate however long you live. Most people have defined contribution plans, which create a finite nest egg to invest. Unfortunately, the egg has to last as long as we do. Many big com-

Helyn Flanagan:
"I Don't Act, Feel, or Think Old"

Tap dance instructor Helyn Flanagan is a woman of "a certain age," and she's the only one who has the certainty about it. Somewhere north of age eighty-five, the Hartford, Connecticut, resident teaches four vigorous tap dancing classes every week to students of all ages and choreographs an annual tap show for them each year. Dancing is the "happiest place I know," she says.

Other than admitting to being "eighty-five-plus," Helyn does not reveal her age. "I don't act, feel, or think old." If people knew her age, she says, "they might treat me differently."

Helyn began teaching dance informally at age eleven and has been at it ever since. In addition to her dance studio, Helyn had a successful career as a professional singer, touring the country for years as a member of a trio called The Modernettes. Even after her singing career tapered off, Helyn continued to teach dance to others—right through a bout with cancer seven years ago. Only three weeks after undergoing surgery, she organized and choreographed the annual student recital she does every year.

"Find out the thing you love most in life and pursue it," Helyn advises. The key, she says, is looking forward—not at old jobs, old hobbies, old lives. "You cannot live on memories— you have to get out and *do*."

panies have frozen their pension plans, saying they cannot afford them, leaving retired employees to shoulder more costs themselves. Cuts in corporate pension benefits are likely to continue. In a recent major accounting survey, half of the companies said that they would consider trimming or freezing plans at some point during 2006.

• The drop in investment returns since the long bull market ended trimmed trillions in paper profits in 401K accounts and lowered expectations that the stock market will see to it that the egg always grows bigger. The average household's invested retirement accounts declined by about 15 percent in the first two years of this century. Those who retired in the late 1990s have had to revisit any assumptions they made about rates of return on investments that are not realistic today.

• Medical costs show no signs of slowing down, with long-term care expenditures projected to triple in real terms over the next forty years as Baby Boomers age and medical costs rise. Companies are trimming health benefits for retirees or dropping the promise of future benefits altogether.

The bottom line for portfolio seekers is this: whether one's financial resources will be adequate is sufficiently clouded by external variables that many people may not be sure which group they fall into. Do they need to work or not?

A PERFECT STORM IN THE WORKPLACE?

The good news is that anyone who wants to work should be able to. The rate at which workers are entering the workforce has fallen from an annual growth rate of almost 3 percent in the 1970s to less than 1 percent today. It is projected to slow to 0.4 percent annually after 2010, and labor economists think growth in the labor force will slip to 0.2 percent for most of the 2020s. On the other side of the equation, over the next fifteen years, about one-fourth of the present workforce will reach sixty-seven, the age (as of 2006, and it's sure to change again) to qualify for full federal retirement benefits. The result will be a crunch that Ira S. Wolfe, a consultant on workforce issues, has termed *the perfect labor storm* (also the name of his book)—a projected shortage of 5.3 million skilled workers by 2010 and 14 million by 2015. Demographics are the main cause. Generation X, those born from 1965 through 1977, is 35 percent smaller than the Baby Boom generation.

Other factors behind the low labor growth rate are that women are no longer surging into the workforce at the same phenomenal rate as during the last quarter century, immigration levels have flattened, and executives are not electing to prolong their careers. For all these reasons, older workers will be in great demand.

There are three implications of this trend for the portfolio approach. One is the opportunity it offers to those who want to work for pay. Many fields and industries will be seeking new workers, but demand will be particularly high for employees with skills not easily replicated, such as those involving judgment, intuition, ethics, inspiration, and imagination. Older workers are primed to fill such spots. Research shows that they have unique problem-solving skills that are difficult to measure on standardized tests.

A second implication of a labor shortage for the portfolio mind-set is the prospect it holds for long-overdue changes in the attitudes toward age in the workplace—a topic addressed at length in Chapter Seven. In order to attract and recruit older workers, companies will have to respond more fully to older workers' preference to ease into retirement through reduced hours and flex-time arrangements. In one study, one-third of full-time workers said they would stay on the job longer than planned if such phased retirement options were offered.

A third implication is how this trend will affect the transfer of knowledge and skills and leadership succession in the American workplace. One-fifth of this country's large companies will be losing 40 percent or more of their most experienced talent—people in top management slots and high-performance executive jobs—in the next five years.

Career Ladder, Career Cycle

A career used to denote an upward, linear progression through an occupation over time. It has become something much more variable, with more pit stops, with second, third, and even fourth careers becoming increasingly common. Two out of five American workers report having had six or more different employers, and worker expectations for how often they will change jobs continue to escalate. And especially in midlife, people are changing not only jobs more often but also occupations. Even among business executives, there is less interest in assuming the corner office. A 2005 study by the global public relations consulting firm Burson-Marsteller found that 54 percent of corporate executives surveyed did not want to lead their companies.

What is behind all this flux? Baby Boomers, predominant among senior-level executives and professionals, have always valued controlling their own destinies, moving in and out of activities based on personal interests and needs. They took this stance to the office, and it has been embraced by their children, the members of Generations X and Y. Companies will have to offer lateral career paths, flex time and benefits, sabbaticals, and job sharing in the workplace to attract the skills they need—and that will make workers in the future even more primed for the portfolio approach.

To gain the utmost control of their destinies, more and more workers are becoming their own bosses. Entrepreneurial activity in the United States peaked in 2000, at the height of the technology-driven economic boom, and then fell, but it has since returned to historically high levels: an estimated 11.5 million Americans are self-employed. This trend will continue, in part because technology makes home offices and telecommuting a realistic and affordable choice. Some fifty million Americans do at least some work from home on a part-time basis. True, basements and barns are not ideal sites from which to compete with large manufacturers or retailers. But thanks in part to new technologies, solo entrepreneurs increasingly can compete with specialized companies in professional services, consulting, and the development of creative products and applications, which is where the growth is in our economy. Americans in extended middle age are playing a leading role in this. Some 5.6 million Americans aged fifty and older are currently self-employed, and one-third of them *started* their own businesses after age fifty.

CULTURAL FACTORS BEHIND THE SHIFT

Many cultural aspects are driving a new way of seeing aging, which supports the pursuit of a life portfolio. Increasingly, older Americans are defining themselves not by their threescore and however many years but by what they do and what their interests are. I see four factors that are prompting people to use their time more thoughtfully.

RISE OF PERSONAL EMPOWERMENT AND CHOICE

People are rejecting the view that we are born with a limited set of choices and increasingly want to decide for themselves about their lives rather than rely on employers, social conventions, or family expectations. They also feel more personally responsible for identifying the choices. This mind-set includes exploring and taking unconventional paths. And it has been augmented by the Internet, which every day is making the hopes, experiences, and plans of people in extended middle age exponentially known to others. Between 2003 and 2005, global Internet usage grew from five hundred to nine hundred million people. One study estimates that two billion people could be online by 2015. The power of such a platform to expose people to new ideas and choices will be enormous.

Boomers are the leaders here, of course. Instead of moving in lockstep sequence from college to the workplace to the golf course, they are straying from the path and re-creating their lives every few years. They try new careers, new hobbies, new cities, and new life roles. In developmental terms, boomers have pioneered cyclical growth rather than the linear path of generations past.

In a recent Merrill Lynch retirement survey, for example, more than half of Baby Boomers expressed a desire not only to continue working but also to change careers. Study author Ken Dychtwald explained it this way: "You have corporate CEOs who want to be schoolteachers and marketing managers who'd really rather run a coffee shop, bookkeepers who want to join the Peace Corps. They'll work fewer hours or only eight months a year, and they won't be as concerned about having the biggest office or the most lucrative job. It will be more important to do something they enjoy." This mind-set aligns perfectly with the portfolio approach, which also is built on the idea of choice, on what is good for us as individuals.

INCREASED DEMAND FOR QUALITY OF LIFE

Sensing that their lives have become busier but not more satisfying, people are paying more attention to quality-of-life concerns, curbing consumption and placing a higher value on personal time. This time is reserved for self-care, including recreation, creative expression, meditation, and spiritual development, as well as for nourishing social connections, such as spending time with one's family or in one's community or working on broader social issues.

The pervasiveness of the spirituality boom and simplicity movement reflects this desire. Other signs are the popularity of life coaches, the abundance of books warning against trying to have it all, and the advent of magazines such as *Real Simple.* Yoga has surged in popularity. In tandem with this desire for balance is an ongoing redefinition of career success and a shift in what people want out of their careers. Increasingly, more really is less! Younger executives and professionals are less work-centric. They are demanding the right to have a life outside the office, which they cite as one of the things they look for in a job.

When they are inside the office, they want more than just a good salary—a concept that experts support as healthy. Studies sponsored by the MacArthur Foundation and the National Institute on Aging show that working not just for income but for meaning and purpose is good for people: 70 percent of sustained physical and mental health in later life can be attributed to lifestyle and environment, and only 30 percent to genes—the inversion of what we long believed to be the case.

IMPACT OF WOMEN ON CULTURAL SHIFTS

Their rate of entry may have dropped, but there are still more women in the U.S. workforce than ever, sixty-six million. Experts say that there could be ninety-two million women workers by 2050. There are also a growing number of women in executive positions. How does this affect portfolio? Women have had to develop flexibility skills to juggle work and family roles, so they tend to be more open to new or alternative ideas in work and life planning. Plus, their new roles have given men an opportunity to catch up in the flexibility department, which they appear to be doing. Research has shown that as more men became full partners at home, taking on more of those responsibilities—even becoming stay-at-home dads—they have been requesting and taking advantage of flexible work arrangements at rates similar to women.

Another implication for portfolio planning is that retirement decisions are no longer limited to just married men (and a good thing, too). This cuts two ways. Having two incomes does give married working couples more flexibility in planning portfolio changes. At the same time, women are often at different stages in their careers and may be less interested in cutting back. Women

Marjory Stoneman Douglas: Late Bloomer

Given Marjory Stoneman Douglas's lead role in saving the Florida Everglades, the White House honor might have come much earlier. But politics does not work that way. So it was not until a full 103 years after her birth in 1890 that Marjory Stoneman Douglas was awarded the Presidential Medal of Freedom.

She smiled as the president put it around her neck.

Douglas lived five more years, dying in 1998 at age 108. "The things I do I do because I'm interested in them," she once said. "I don't like to be bored. I can't understand old people who can't find anything to do when there's so much left to be done."

A tireless environmentalist, Douglas is best known as the primary force behind the state and federal laws protecting Florida's wetlands. But she didn't take up that cause until after a long and successful career as a journalist, short story author, and teacher.

At age 57, she wrote the definitive call to arms on the subject, *The Everglades: River of Grass;* at 58, she went on a public speaking tour; at 79, she founded the watchdog group Friends of the Everglades; at 89, she addressed the Florida state senate about the drainage and pollution of the Everglades; and at 103, she received her medal at the White House. Douglas said that she owed her achievements to perseverance. "If people haven't heard me, it isn't my fault," she quipped.

typically enter the workforce later: most new female workers are between age forty-five and fifty-four. Having essentially just started their careers, these women are unlikely candidates for extended tours in a Winnebago.

INCREASING INTERGENERATIONAL CONNECTION

As more people work past traditional retirement age, the workforce is becoming increasingly multigenerational. Although this can create tensions (according to the Society for Human Resource Management, 58 percent of large companies say they deal with generational conflicts), there are more positive aspects.

Older workers who try new roles at work regardless of their previous position show younger people the value of nonlinear careers and nonretirement outlooks. But Generations X and Y also have plenty to teach: they already tend to view work as one piece in a lifestyle. They may be less oriented to job security than social mobility and fulfillment—an approach that aligns well with the portfolio mentality.

The trend extends beyond the workplace. Retirement communities are cropping up on American college campuses. Currently, sixty colleges or universities have campus-linked retirement communities, which offer the opportunity for rich interaction and learning across generations. Residents say that purchasing spots in these communities buys you more than just a home or condo—it buys you a lifestyle. Residents can enroll in classes, but they can also interact with students outside the classroom on projects and in recreational time. One-third of residents attend football games.

People are also connecting across generations within families, as grandparents become more involved with and connected to their grandchildren. The average age at which Americans become grandparents is around fifty, which means they have several decades to teach to, and learn from, their grandchildren. The number of two- and three-generation households is growing fast, according to the U.S. Census Bureau. Interaction with grandkids keeps people young and active. As a promotion for *Grand* magazine's 2004 premier issue said, "Yesterday's grandparents rocked on the porch. But today's baby boomer grandparents really rock." Magazines like *Grand* are just one of many outlets that boomers are using to connect with their grandchildren. Internet-based family Web sites are another. There is also evidence that having grandchildren is prompting older people to create more balanced lives—ones that include more leisure time. Whether in a workplace or an academic or family environment, people are using a portfolio outlook to connect with other generations—an experience that can only be enriching for all involved.

"Aging Is a Metaphor for Living"

Below are excerpts from a conversation I had with Joseph Coughlin, the founder and head of the Massachusetts Institute of Technology's AgeLab, an innovative, multidisciplinary research center to identify and develop public-private solutions around aging. Founded in 1999, it was the first center to integrate research in fields including gerontology, behavior health, psychology, technology, engineering, and political science.

David Corbett: Why was AgeLab founded?

There's a real shortfall in what we've done as a society. We've spent billions of dollars and billions of labor hours to enable us to live longer. Life expectancy in 1900 was somewhere around forty-seven and maybe a little bit higher in Europe, and with improvements in childhood health and sanitation, it began to rise steadily. Today it is around seventy-eight in the United States. Medicine and health technology tend to get much of the credit, although if you look at it in historical terms, it was really more civil engineering works, like cleaner water, that enabled us to live longer. So the next question is, what are we going to do? We don't have what I call the *infrastructure of an aging society.* Over the past five or six decades, aging's been defined around health and financial security. So we have the medical systems (some would argue we don't even have those in place, but I think they're in decent shape) and people thinking about their financial situations for the future. But I saw that there was no real infrastructure of aging to help you do all the things that you did as a younger person, to come and go when you want, where you want, why you want. The ability to "age in place" in your own home for as long as you wish, as independently as you wish, is a prospect that right

(Continued)

now is quite dubious for most people. We're working on how to engage aging people to become productive members of society. One way is to continue contributing through work. For better or worse, many of us find personal meaning out of our work. But it's also about enabling us as a society, as we age, to continue to be active in our various domains—home, workplace, and everywhere else.

Corbett: Why hasn't more happened?

We're trapped in a mind-set of what we think aging is about. We still define aging around what we thought aging was about in, say, 1964, or maybe even before. And that was defining old as anything over sixty, being alone, poor, and being in ill health. And for some, that is the case. But the fact is, we now have a population where, to quote an AARP magazine cover, sixty is the new thirty. So we need to recalibrate our vision of what is old, what our expectations are, and then part of the AgeLab's vision is to really create the groundwork and the infrastructure to enable—and this is our moon-shot vision, if you will—a hundred years of quality living.

Corbett: What should people be thinking about?

They should be thinking about things beyond where the business of retirement is today—baseline health insurance, health coverage, financial security. But if you are fortunate to live ten, twenty, thirty, forty years beyond retirement, what are you going to do? Start asking yourself not just are you going to go golfing, because you'll speak to many folks who have enough of that after a week, but are you going to continue to learn? Do you want to retire to change careers rather than simply retire? What are the things you have to do to make that happen? Where are you living? For instance, if you're living in the suburbs—and that might be quite grand, and that's where 70 percent of the population has chosen to be—that's great. But if for some reason, you're no longer willing or able to drive, now what? So really start planning how you can keep your life as seamless tomorrow as it is today. One thing about aging that is incomprehensible to me is why we personally, publicly, and business-wise don't plan ahead, because aging is one of the few things that when you do strategic planning, you can plot out on a chart and say that the problem and the opportunity are already alive today. And with most cases, they *will* be here in twenty or thirty years. So it's one of the few factors or variables that you can actually say, I know that this is going to be here. Technology is always a prayer, economics is a hope, all the other things that one uses to do strategic planning. And yet, all those folks who are forecasting a dismal future because of the aging population, rather than celebrating the great achievement of humankind—that is, roughly thirty more years of living as compared to a hundred years ago—they are saying how terrible it's going to be. So if we don't take it as an opportunity and an urgent challenge, it is likely it will be the killer of productivity, pension funds, and health care that many are making a business out of forecasting.

Corbett: What surprises people about the research you're doing at AgeLab, what you've learned about aging?

If you look at people who've done the New England Centenarian Study on living to a hundred or George Vaillant's study on aging well, attitude and a sense of humor seem to be bigger predictors of how well you're going to age than even your genetics. People are surprised, especially young people, that aging begins a lot earlier than we think it does. Typically, people tend to think that aging begins ten to twenty years older than they are. But studies show that cognitive function begins to change in

(Continued)

your late thirties. Flexibility begins to decline markedly in the mid-forties. . . . It actually starts a lot sooner, both on a physiological, a cognitive, and even an attitude level. So aging comes sooner than we like, and the speed with which the world is changing is making even the very young only very temporarily able-bodied. Knowledge is moving, technology is moving, institutions—entire governments and economies are changing at lightning speed. So age is no longer a chronological definition; age is more a state of mind. Really, if we have any impact here at the Lab, we'll no longer talk in terms of young or old, we'll simply talk about living—how well you're living. Aging is a metaphor for living. And yet most people don't want to hear the *age* word. I can't tell you how many people loathe the word *aging* and the name of my lab. It drives them nuts! So there's a reason I should change it, but part of why I want to keep it is also a good reason: if you're two, you're age two; if you're a hundred, you're age a hundred. So the alternative to aging is not nearly as pretty.

CHAPTER FOUR

PORTFOLIO LIFE

I introduced the Life Portfolio Program twelve years ago, when I sensed a palpable restlessness among successful men and women in their fifties and sixties. They no longer wanted their careers to be front and center, but they felt they were too young to retire. Unfortunately, too many of them saw only those two options: full-time continual work or full-time continual retirement. I saw our program as a creative alternative to that dilemma. Our starting point then, as now, is that retirement is a process, not an event, and that with planning and a desire to live authentically, it could be enriching.

Two things happen as people shift from career perspective to portfolio perspective. They begin to take a broader view of their lives, beyond defining themselves in terms of their work. And they learn to pay attention to the issue of balance, to the interplay of parts that make up a whole life. Typical is David Ellis of Boston, the former chief executive officer of Boston's Museum of Science and a former president of Lafayette College in Pennsylvania, who has been pursuing a half dozen diverse interests and projects since retiring. "My portfolio life is great," he said. "It's been a chance to look at life from a broad point of view, rather than the narrow perspectives I had while running the museum and Lafayette."

Portfolio responds to a calling that is knit into the fabric of our very being. It is about what our motivators are, what makes us feel most alive. Portfolio development is what our true work should be, for it's where our deep gifts, and our gladness, meet the needs of the world.

By the way, while advancing the *life portfolio* idea has become something of a personal mission, the term is not unique to me. In the early 1990s, British economist Charles Handy noticed the rise of part-time, contract, and consulting work in place of traditional employment. He advised people not to think of themselves as having a continuous career but rather a "portfolio of jobs" over a lifetime. As a life-planning tool, the portfolio concept borrows from financial services the idea of a balanced mix of asset allocations, all working together toward a long-term goal. The allocations we consider as we build a life portfolio are the ways we invest our time and energy. We identify five such elements, as shown in Figure 4.1: (1) work or income production, (2) intellectual stimulation and spiritual self-development, (3) recreation, (4) cultivating connections to family and friends, and (5) giving back through humanitarian or community engagement.

CREATING A LONG-TERM PERSPECTIVE

In the program we offer at New Directions, clients go through a substantial assessment or, put another way, a process of self-discovery, leading to new goals. They then explore opportunities through

FIGURE 4.1. LIFE PORTFOLIO ALLOCATION MODEL.

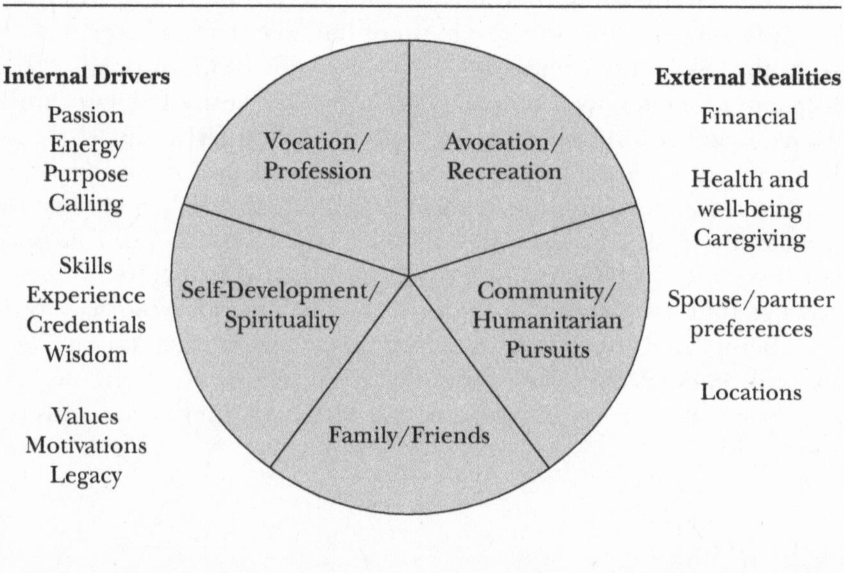

Internal Drivers

Passion
Energy
Purpose
Calling

Skills
Experience
Credentials
Wisdom

Values
Motivations
Legacy

Vocation/Profession

Avocation/Recreation

Self-Development/Spirituality

Community/Humanitarian Pursuits

Family/Friends

External Realities

Financial

Health and well-being
Caregiving

Spouse/partner preferences

Locations

networking, personal research, and what we call *experiencing the space*. Finally, in consultation with their chosen team of personal advisers, they select pursuits, practices, or goals in each of these five elements. We try to keep goals and desires aligned, which we have found to be a practical recipe for success. Our division of the portfolio lifestyle into five areas is admittedly somewhat arbitrary, but the ones we use do seem to be core components of a full life. Significantly, alternating among the different mind-sets that these elements require helps us recharge inwardly. Don't ask me the brain science. I just know it works. It is also a way to keep our long-term perspective on what is most important to us.

Balance is essential to the notion of a life portfolio. As you allocate your time to vocational-professional pursuits, self-development, avocations, time with family and friends, and giving back, you balance a commitment to any one of these against the others. The real challenge is to find the combination that expresses your identity and goals. It is not just a matter of balancing the number of hours allocated but of comparing and contrasting the value you draw from different pursuits. Those activities that permit you to make a fuller contribution of your gifts or use a fuller range of your skills might have more value to you than others.

We originally called the new concept our Three-Four Program, meaning work three days a week and play four. But the notion was too confining. "Don't lock me into any routine at this point in my life," some clients said. "I want flexibility." More important, the label did not suggest the broader ideal of a balanced life. It did not convey ongoing learning, personal and spiritual growth, giving back, and possible legacies. Something else was needed, and the notion of single company-centered careers being replaced by employee-managed portfolios of jobs began to emerge in business circles. Why not take that term beyond jobs and apply it to our whole lives, I thought.

At the time, about 1994, we conceived of the portfolio process as a new stage in the three-stage pattern Americans had followed since World War II. That was the sequence I grew up with: you get an education, then you work your butt off, and then you retire, during which time you get monthly checks, do little, and die. Portfolio was our new third stage in a four-stage cycle, our own variation on what is sometimes called *pre-retirement*.

However, my thinking shifted about portfolio a few years ago. It was not a prelude or period *between* career and retirement, I realized, but a long-term approach to living a balanced, vital life for the remainder of our natural lives. Like a financial portfolio, a life portfolio must be rebalanced from time to time, as external conditions change or as new goals and objectives emerge. Time spent on income production, for example, may decrease as we age (or conversely, it may increase with new opportunities), and allocation to other *time investments* may similarly change. Retirement used to be an event. Portfolio is an adaptable process that goes on as long as we do, which is why I say it replaces retirement. With that recognition, it then seemed to me that we had gone from three stages, to four stages, and now back again to just three: education, career, and portfolio. Retirement disappeared.

My thinking on portfolio changed again somewhat as I wrote this book. I see it more and more as a *lifelong* way of thinking, not something bound by age or a certain stage of life. Yes, the period from age fifty to one's middle seventies and beyond can be a kind of liberation or second adolescence, a time when people can take back their own lives. A portfolio perspective can help advance that. But why should any of us lose our lives to begin with?

In the portfolio mind-set, we ask ourselves these questions: What unique gifts do I have that I can now actualize? What will enable me to feel at journey's end that I have not just visited this world but have lived a full life? I concede that in the hectic career and family-building phase, there is often little time or desire to reflect on such questions. There is money to make, children to nurture, houses to buy, and careers to advance. But if people in their twenties, thirties, and forties could keep these questions alive at least in the backs of their minds, then, I believe, fewer Americans would get to the second half of life feeling a need to reclaim their true identities.

The notion that people need to think about the meaning and purpose of what they are doing with their lives *all along the way,* rather than saving it for a kind of retirement project, is growing. One person who advocates this is David Ellis, whom I just mentioned. "Schools and universities need new attitudes about helping people think about their postcareer years while they are still young,"

Why a Life *Portfolio*?

Portfolio is an apt term for the mind-set and lifestyle replacing the concept of retirement. The origin of the word helps explain why. A *folio* is a sheet of paper folded in half to make two leaves with four surfaces. By writing on folios and stitching them together, Romans made the first book (which they called a *codex*). After Gutenberg, the folio came to mean an early printed book of a certain size. The largest sheet of paper that printers could feed through their press was designated a folio. It cost more money, so it was used for expensive, prestigious volumes. By the seventeenth century, folio came to mean any large, noteworthy book, such as the *First Folio of William Shakespeare*.

The *port* prefix is the root of numerous words that suggest the movement or transfer of things. (Canoes are *port*able, but if you have to *port*age one to a sea*port,* you can't ask a *port*er to do it.) Hence, portfolio first came to mean a leather carrying case of important documents, literally a portable book. Over time, it came to mean something that reflects who you are. Artists have portfolios of their works; diplomats are said to have portfolios of duties. Your portfolio represents your work, your interests, what you have done—it represents who you are.

Then there's the financial meaning of portfolio. A portfolio of investments builds on the same notion of binding things together. It is a collection of invested assets. In order to manage risk and seize opportunities for profit whichever way the market winds blow, one must have an investment portfolio allocated into diversified sectors. Diversification and allocation involve a balance of elements and a sense of perspective (concepts are especially useful when we reallocate our portfolios). In my view, all of these principles are central to the life-planning approach that can help us make the most out of *all* of life. Our life portfolio is an agenda we will always have with us.

this former college president says. Currently, he adds, they are not creating enough curricula or informal studies to encourage people to plan. Ellis says that teaching preconceived plans is not needed and would not work. But students could learn the value and the mental habit of flexibility and curiosity in life planning—flexibility to make adjustments as they execute life plans and curiosity to try new ideas and paths as they get older.

Another believer is former *New York Times* columnist William Safire, whom I mentioned in Chapter Two. People, he wrote in his final column, on January 24, 2005, should be "laying the basis for future activities in the midst of current careers." The payoff, he wrote, is being able to "seize an exhilarating second wind" in life. Safire is a case in point. He left the *Times* after thirty-two years and more than three thousand columns at age seventy-five—not to retire but to begin a new full-time career as chairman and chief executive of the Dana Foundation, which promotes learning about and scientific research on the brain.

"Never let yourself vegetate," Safire advised his readers in his last blast as an op-ed page columnist (Safire's language column in the Sunday magazine continues). "Your brain needs exercise or it will atrophy. Extending the life of the body means nothing unless we also extend the life of the mind." The columnist said people should select a future career in their late thirties or early forties. They should find something that interests them, engages their skills, and reflects their knowledge. Then they should spend years learning about it and let it develop into their full-time vocation sometime in their sixties. It was encouraging to me personally to see a major nationally syndicated newspaper columnist use his parting space to tell people to think ahead about some of the issues we deal with in our portfolio program.

PIONEERING THE IDEA

The portfolio perspective is not new, of course. People chose to adopt the main elements of a portfolio lifestyle long before anyone thought of using that term. One of them is Al McNeilly, who is eighty-five years old. If you walk by his house in Owl's Head, Maine, you may find a sign that says, in the local lingo for lobstering, "Gone Hauling." That means he is out on his boat, perhaps pulling up by hand one of his forty-two lobster traps, each of which can weigh up to fifty pounds.

Born in 1921, Al had his college years interrupted by Army Air Corps service in World War II; he flew thirty-four missions as the navigator of a B-29 bomber. He graduated from the University of Maine in 1947, and after pitching one season in the minor leagues he worked in a gas station for the old Esso Oil Company. He then was promoted to the position of manager of wholesale and industrial business, Exxon Company USA, Houston, in 1966. By the time he retired in 1981, Al had turned that division into a powerhouse of profits.

Succeeding at a major multinational corporation like Exxon may not encourage people to think about life beyond one's career, but Al was different. His love of Maine and sense of belonging there never left him and caused him to do something few executives did in the "organization man" era of the 1960s. When Exxon moved him to Houston, he was able to gain extra time off each year to return to Maine "as part of the deal." Maine stayed with him in his mind, even in Houston. When he appeared before the board of directors in 1980 to announce his division's record profits, he set off a concealed marine horn under the table that popped a few buttons on his listeners' suits.

Today, Al lives a stone's throw from where he grew up, in a house with a widow's walk that looks down on the harbor and his boat. He "hosts" at the town's general store, serves on the boards of the University of Maine Aging Center, the Owl's Head Transportation Museum, the University of Maine Alumni Association, a local hospital, the historical society, and a shelter for children. He's also involved in an initiative called The Atlantic Challenge, a foundation that teaches marine craftsmanship to troubled youth.

Most of all, Al is a Mainer and a lobsterman. And don't ask him if it is a hobby. I made that mistake, and he gave me a long injured look before he broke into a smile. "No," he said. "I work at it as if it was the last dollar I ever earned." Al says he "competes" with the other lobstermen.

The key to his successful retirement, he says, is that he *didn't* retire. He just changed what he was doing, following earlier loves. And he remained engaged. "What I would tell people my age is you have to be involved. Try like the devil to live on the positive side of everything. Too many people live on 'the glass is half empty' side. The glass is fuller than you think."

COMMON PORTFOLIO PATHS

Creating a middle way between a full-time job that no longer satisfies and full-time retirement was not hard for Al, because he never really gave up his other interests and passions, including his love of Maine, during the years he worked for Exxon. But the transition does pose a challenge to many people, especially those who have had pressure-cooker jobs.

We recommend a systematic step-by-step process to design a life portfolio, which I will lay out in the chapters ahead. In brief, people continue to work to produce income but on their own terms, often in part-time or interim situations. Three common paths to producing income in the portfolio approach are consulting, board directorships, and working in the nonprofit arena. A common thread in the choice of work is that the best opportunities are generated within. In a true portfolio perspective, you know what you have to offer and want to do, and then you create a demand for it.

Some individuals start new businesses. That takes more time, but we have seen clients do it in tune with the overall portfolio principle of balance. Others turn to teaching, writing, speaking, investing in small businesses, launching family foundations, and serving in various charitable or humanitarian efforts.

I have witnessed fascinating transformations among our portfolio clients. A former vice chairman of a bank runs a cemetery. A former technology executive with a lifelong interest in history is now a guide at Monticello, the home of President Thomas Jefferson. (His big thrill was getting a library card admitting him to the National Archives. "I feel like a kid again," he said.) A former mutual fund manager raises alpacas (looks like a llama) in New Hampshire, and a former career military officer raises sheep.

Dick Broussard is typical. Once a public affairs officer for the Army Corps of Engineers, he now drives a school bus in rural Vermont as part of his portfolio. Dick says he loves listening to the chatter of his charges, who range from kindergarten through twelfth grade, as he drives them across broad vistas, up winding roads, and over mountains. He says he also finds time between his morning and afternoon trips to run, hike, or paddle the Connecticut River in his canoe. He is also sexton of his town church and volunteers at a homeless shelter.

The portfolio life of another engineer, a former officer of a technology firm, is centered on his two foster care children. This man claims he has "gone soft" and "done a 180" in terms of his personality. I don't believe that. I think he is just letting himself do what he always wanted.

Choosing activities in sync with our true selves can revitalize our mental and physical health, our personal and family relationships, and our sense of purpose in life. With luck, it will also help our wallets. But it's important to remember that creating a life portfolio is not just an exercise in lifestyle management. At its heart, portfolio means learning how to sort out what is important to us; it means comparing one thing with another and rating its importance to us personally. It also means paying attention to one's values and to the unfinished business of life.

A New Role for Family

For many, that unfinished business includes deepening or repairing connections to and relationships with important people in our lives. People in the portfolio mind-set often do this, I have found, within their own families. I talked earlier about the assessment process as "Me 101." While taking that "course," one can start developing the notion of oneself as the "CEO of Me, Inc." If that stands up, then maybe a person's family represents the "Incorporated," the "company" the chief executive reports to. That viewpoint recognizes families remain our chief support systems, guideposts, and sources of meaning.

One of the good things that happens in the portfolio part of life is that the family tends to replace the corporation as the institution demanding the most energy and ultimate loyalty.

I recall a man I met who came to such a realization in a roundabout way. He had been a chief financial officer in his late fifties, and I met him after he lost his job as the result of a merger. He faced a decision between taking one more job or moving into a portfolio lifestyle. We were talking one day, and I must have been going on about my view of families. After a while, he interrupted me.

"Well, that's great for you, Dave, but we don't have any kids," he said.

This threw me. I thought for a moment and said, "Well, do you have any siblings, nephews, or nieces?"

"Yes, I have a niece I've always been fond of—actually I'm her godfather—but we've lost touch since she moved to Phoenix."

I asked what the niece was doing in Phoenix. The man said she had started her own company. I was told, "It's doing great, except that she doesn't know how to keep the books and she is worried about that." I could almost see the lightbulb go on in his head. "Jeez," he said after a pause. "Here I am a CFO, and I have a niece who needs help with her company's finances, and I haven't even called her recently." A few days later, I got a phone call from him. He had decided not to go after a job but take the portfolio route. And he was getting on a plane that day to go to Phoenix.

Another person who took care of some important business at a turning point in life is Bob Williams. Bob worked for the State Street Bank for thirty years, much of it in overseas banking, including a stint in Asia. In 2003, when Bob was fifty-five years old, the bank offered an attractive voluntary separation package. Bob had not anticipated leaving the bank for another five years and had not done much planning. "I'm not a golfer, and I didn't really want to stop working, but I also knew that I would be transitioning out anyway," he said. "Also, I think if you work for a corporation, no matter how happy you are in your job, and I was fairly happy, you still have a desire for independence, for change. So I thought, why not leave now and do something I really want to do?" he said.

Bob took the offer and soon found himself at home during the day, a disorienting experience for a senior executive who had traveled extensively. His first act? He sat down and wrote by hand a five-page letter to his wife, his spouse for thirty years. "I wrote out all the things I should have said for years and didn't," including acknowledging that he had not always put his family first. "I told her how much I love her, and how I was looking forward to spending more time with her, and with our daughter, and deepening our relationship."

Bob admits that he took a wrong turn after his early retirement. As an independent corporate finance consultant, he succeeded in helping a troubled company recapitalize itself. But then he accepted a full-time job for the company, which he quit a year later when he realized that another full-time job was not what he wanted.

Bob's current life offers a pretty good window onto the possibilities of the portfolio approach. He serves as a director on two corporate boards to "keep one foot in my field of expertise" and is studying Mandarin Chinese at Harvard. He volunteers at the local YMCA and, being a licensed pilot, became involved in the all-volunteer emergency transport group called Angel Flight. Williams also makes a lot of time for his family. "I took a day recently and took a nephew who loves motorcycles to a bike show in New Hampshire. He loved it, and we had a ball. That was something I would never have even thought of doing before."

Like any transition, the transition into the portfolio attitude takes conscious effort. It takes slowing down, decompressing, taking

"Who can say? I suppose I'm as happy as my portfolio will allow me to be."

Source: Cartoonbank, all rights reserved. Published in *The New Yorker,* June 8, 1987.

in new inputs and perspectives, and trusting one's instincts. This is not always easy. To be excited by the new possibilities ahead, to some extent we must be able to let go of our prior career mentality and lifestyle.

A lawyer I know spent thirty years at a top law firm, rising to managing partner. He spent his first year in retirement not thinking about new horizons but wondering how he would get through the day. It wasn't that he lacked projects; he had a long list on a yellow legal pad. It was that he felt too alone and disoriented, too sad, really, to bring his good energy to bear on his new life. "When I lost my role at the firm, I lost all sense of community," he told me. "I was miserable about that for the better part of a year."

Another client was a senior executive of global manufacturing at Digital Equipment Corporation in its glory days, then codirected the Leaders for Manufacturing Program at the Massachusetts Institute of Technology. Life after MIT posed challenges for him as well—including discovering how deeply ingrained the concept of the workweek was in his mind. "It is a completely different perspective," said William Hanson, who lives on Cape Cod. "It's like I had been a right-handed golfer all my life, and now I had to learn how to swing left-handed."

SOMETHING THAT WILL OUTLAST US

One of the questions people confront in the portfolio perspective is what kind of legacy they will leave the world. A legacy is the mark, the enduring stamp of our lives. It's what endures after the journey's end. It can have a concrete form, such as an artistic creation, a social program, or a financial gift that helps others. But legacies are also created when people transmit their values and beliefs to future generations. The psychologist and philosopher Williams James expressed it well. "The great use of life," he wrote, "is to spend it for something that will outlast us."

A real legacy is freely given. It's also a testament that takes time to be felt, a kind of aftereffect of what we have done and given in our lives. In my book, legacies are inextricably linked to our values. A legacy represents something you believed in, something you found worth working on or fighting for. Legacies happen when we respond authentically to our callings.

Creating a legacy can be complicated by the temptation to use it for self-aggrandizement or to meet a desire for recognition. Others may even see it as a way to circumvent the finality of death. But that is not what I mean by legacy. Perhaps in thinking about legacy, we should remember the Roman orator and politician Cato the Elder. He wrote that he would prefer that future Romans would recall his life and wonder why there was *no* monument to him—rather than to see one and wonder why it was there.

My own legacy is as much a work in progress as it is for anyone. One small contribution I feel good about is knowing that our portfolio program has helped people gain not only new life-planning skills but also a new sense of hope and possibility about their own life dreams.

That was the sense I got from a letter that Perry McIntosh of Salem, Massachusetts, sent me last year. Perry had been a publishing executive for many years. Then, in midlife, she chose to enter our Life Portfolio Program a couple years ago. She is now an independent writer, editor, and inventor of novelty products, one of which she succeeded in bringing to market and is enjoying some success with. It is a gift item for cat lovers—a mouse discreetly mounted trophy-style on a wood frame.

As a result of her creating a life portfolio, "I've developed the skills, courage, and contacts to fulfill a lifelong dream of bringing some of my inventions to market," she wrote. Describing herself as a professional woman who had followed a conventional career path, she added, "I'm sure I would not have seized on the opportunities inherent in transition if not for the portfolio concept."

Ultimately, portfolio is about making the individual parts of our lives serve the larger goal of living a productive, meaningful, and happy life. And, as I mentioned, it is something we should think about and work on *throughout the course* of our lives. The key is being intentional about it. Ask yourself, Is this what I want my one life to be about? What am I uniquely suited to do that will give me a complete sense of having fully lived? What will I remember and treasure about my life's journey? If, even as we build families and careers, we could keep alive at least some of the questions of the portfolio approach, perhaps fewer people would get to their fifties and sixties needing to dig out or unearth their true identities.

CHAPTER FIVE

STEPS TOWARD PORTFOLIO

How does one create a life portfolio? No single path suits everyone. Portfolios are planned months or years in advance but also arise from sudden or unexpected events that require individuals to plan (or adapt plans) on the fly. People develop life portfolios by seizing opportunities and acting decisively—but also by testing the waters, watching and listening over time. They may "wean" their way from career mode to portfolio, a process I will explain in this chapter. Portfolios are designed with the help of sophisticated assessment tools, such as our matrix of personal motivators. But they also arise when individuals take a leap of faith. A life portfolio may center on doing new things in new arenas, or it may chiefly involve an individual's building on what he or she has always done best.

A life portfolio is dynamic as well as individualized, so it may shift in ways you did not expect. And it also must be rebalanced on a periodic basis as you go forward. I explained the basic idea of a life portfolio in the last chapter, and I elaborate on how to create one in Chapters Eight through Fifteen. These cover engaging in an assessment, acquiring a new frame of mind, planning, putting your plan into action, and avoiding known pitfalls, with specific tools or pointers in each area. It seems useful here, however, to preview in broad strokes the core steps and stages in the process to help you envision it in a practical perspective.

I believe in planning. I think the "ideal" situation is one in which people become aware of a desire to transition from full-time work and start to investigate what might come next. In this blue-sky, exploratory stage, you try to identify needs that you have and lay the groundwork for long-term planning. One important first step is to get your immediate family—spouse, partner, children—deeply involved. Learn what their expectations are and review any commitments they have or that you have made to them that might impinge on the process. If you are contemplating a move, this is a good time for early conversations about location.

It's important as you become more committed to the process to go beyond daydreaming. You will make more progress if you have a flexible but real way of exploring or developing new commitments to begin to replace what you are leaving behind. It helps you to allocate time for planning, to create a schedule and stick to it.

Even though I advocate planning, I recognize the reality that not everybody has the luxury to plan. An event occurs, such as the loss of a job or a sudden opportunity that would not have been possible to consider or plan for. Some people simply do not have the psychological temperament to plan well in advance.

We see both people who have thought about their portfolios long in advance and those more or less caught in a swirl of events. Although no one prefers the latter situation, in some ways being *thrust* into change is easier. You are not agonizing over how to leave a full-time job: it left you. One of the hardest challenges for people mulling a major change is deciding that *now* is the time to bail out, to begin a process of transition. In that scenario, having your back up against the wall can be a great motivator.

Weaning

There is a middle ground between these two styles of transition, which is the principle of *weaning*. It addresses the reality that personal change is often extremely hard—which, unfortunately, is why many people never attempt it. It can seem overwhelming. How to start? Rushing at a life change does not work. Most of the time, we cannot make a giant leap to where we need to go. So we break it down and go at it little by little, bit by bit. Change is ultimately a zigzag process of small, experimental steps that increase your confidence, focus, and commitment.

We call this weaning. I first heard the term used about moving from a career to a life portfolio by a client who had been a senior partner at a national law firm. "The firm was like a narcotic," he said. "I tried to leave 'cold turkey' once, and I was back in six months. This time, I was more deliberate. I really set out to wean myself away."

Another client who had been with one company for thirty-five years told me, "Weaning from Mother Ship was one of the hardest things I ever did." That was several years ago, and I know that he still struggles with this issue from time to time. But when he had to do it, he accomplished the separation by withdrawing bit by bit over the better part of a year.

Wean literally means to get a baby animal to stop suckling and take other food. Any farmer or parent knows how hard this can be. The solution? A slow, consistent process of substitution. We also speak of people weaning themselves of an undesirable habit or interest.

Weaning into portfolio is scaling back so we can move into a relaxed, creative zone. It is incremental. It's a work in process, one day, one week, and one month at a time. We have to learn to trust the process. Weaning ourselves from the security of W2 tax forms to the entrepreneurial mentality required by 1099 self-employment forms, for example, takes time.

Clients sometimes ask me about the possible outcomes or probability of success in their change. They are just a little anxious, and they want a peek at what the results might be. I tell them that the journey is the destination. This is something I have come to believe

Tips on How to Wean

- Plan when and how you will begin your transition. Don't hold it in. Share your explorations. Get buy-in from your family.
- Consider which "old priorities" to let go to make room for new agendas.
- Subscribe to newspapers, magazines, and professional or trade journals in your new areas of interest.
- Think about endings. Endings release energy tied up by old arrangements. Endings can return us to parts of our lives that have been missing, or to emptiness, which is where creativity begins.

deeply: *manage the process well, and the results will take care of them-selves. Ignore the process, and you may not have any results.*

When does weaning begin? At the very outset, casual one-on-one conversations with friends or mentors who have already entered portfolio can be a good way to start a person thinking. Such conversations are casual, no commitments required. They are simply a way for people who have known only careers to learn more about this huge new world.

Some people in our portfolio program anticipate leaving their primary careers but have not actually done so. The weaning begins when they go to part-time or begin the assessment. Afterward, when goals are made and plans are started, they step up the more formal process of leaving. Other clients have separated from prior careers or commitments by anywhere from three months to three years. Still others, as I have said, are being driven forward by external events. It may be too late for this latter group to wean *from* former jobs, but it's never too late to wean consciously *into* the portfolio process.

People wean from careers to portfolios in different stages and for different reasons. We may have to slowly and consciously back away from the value we have placed on money and title, a lifelong concept of success that no longer serves. A friend told us, "You need to leave your wallet and ego at the door."

The whole process can be a bit like going to a movie. You enter the bright lobby, buy your ticket and popcorn, and step into the dark theater. It's a harsh adjustment; it takes time to see clearly as you grope for a seat. You may feel not in control. But then you see the little aisle lights: faint, reassuring guides. These lights have weaned you from the lobby to the movie. We should be looking for signal lights pointing us forward as we go through any transition.

Weaning can also simply begin after an intuition, a feeling, or an emotional need for change. The very recognition of a desire for change often helps trigger the process. Pay attention to what does and what does not feel right. Follow your hunches. "There is a time for departure," says a character in a play by Tennessee Williams, "even when there's no certain place to go."

If you sense that that time is at hand, begin to wean your attention away from the needs of your employer to yourself. Start to look in the mirror and take inventory of your old and new talents,

Peter Harris: Gone to the Dogs

Peter Harris worked twenty-six years for one accounting firm during his first career. He made partner by age thirty-one, but in his late forties he hit a wall. Promoted sideways and asked to yield his status as an equity partner, Peter faced a choice. After realizing that he was not happy and could live on less than he was making, he came to New Directions as a client in our Life Portfolio Program.

His life has gone to the dogs since then. But Peter's happy about it, and so are we.

During his assessment, Peter found that he wanted to rebalance his professional, volunteer, and family time. He worked this into his portfolio plan. To produce income, he became a part-time consultant on state and local tax issues. He also volunteers, together with his wife, to help run a summer camp that reunites siblings in foster care who live apart from each other during the year.

But the part of his life portfolio that got his sense of purpose was greyhounds. Peter, a lifelong dog lover, learned that greyhounds are often put to sleep when their racing days are over. He decided to adopt two former racers and to train them for "pet therapy" for people in institutionalized care.

Peter brings the dogs to nursing homes and other facilities. He stands by a patient's bedside or wheelchair as they touch, caress, and talk to the animals. Contact with animals improves the emotional health of hospital and institutional patients. "Alzheimer's patients connect with the dogs as they pet them," Peter said. "There seems to be some kind of emotional linking that happens."

"It's a win-win-win proposition. The greyhounds have gone from a kennel to a loving home, the elders whom we visit are thrilled to spend time with the dogs, and I know that I've helped make the day brighter for others."

Peter sets aside one afternoon a week for pet therapy, which has become a priority on his busy calendar. The nursing homes and adult care facilities he visits are a far cry from the polished precincts of a corporate accounting giant. That's fine with Peter, who calls his new venture hectic but fun and exciting. "Plus," he added, "I don't think I'll ever retire. I'll just change the mix of the portfolio activities."

interests, values, and personal beliefs. Try to look at these through the lens of your current personal situation as well as updated external realities. This is the beginning of the assessment process described in Chapter Eight.

Assessment is all about self-discovery. It can be as rigorous a process as you want it to be, but even a flexible approach should include serious input from and sharing with others. Planning particular pursuits, affiliations, and roles comes later in the process. During the early stage of assessment, we focus more on the environments and general conditions and types of activities that are important to us.

Sometimes clients come to us who feel burned out from previous pursuits and are intent on doing something new. That can be great. But I also advise people with that attitude to consider "mining" their own experience to look for gold in their own backyard. Rarely is a life portfolio created anew out of whole cloth. It almost always reflects some continuity. Assessment is critical in that case, for it helps show people what they have done well that they can build on.

A PERSONAL BOARD OF ADVISERS

A life portfolio begins with an internal commitment to change. No one can do that but you, and that commitment alone can generate progress. But the process cannot come to fruition without the help of others. You are fooling yourself if you think new paths in life are created in vacuums. Family, friends, and work colleagues have much to contribute and can function as allies and supporters during the process. For this reason, we recommend that people entering the portfolio process ask a spectrum of people who know them well to serve on what we call a *personal board of advisers*.

The group or circle is really a sounding board. These boards include people from your past and present, those who know you from your work and those who relate to you more personally. Sharing what you are thinking or feeling with them is important: advisers advise best when they feel connected to your ideas and thoughts.

In most cases, these advisers are your close friends and your family. But this varies, depending on individual situations. Personality factors also come into play. Some find it easy to reach out, whereas others have a stronger preference to go it alone. They may find reaching out difficult. In such a case, a professional coach might help. A coach can be useful in the way that having someone help you with financial planning is important. Most people like to have a second opinion, someone to validate the decisions they have made or to help uncover new possibilities.

A tricky part is defining your relationship to a personal board of advisers. It is best to approach your board in a slightly more structured way than you would do with close friends you might invite to your house to socialize. Those who know you well may have a hard time looking in an open-minded way at your options or offering critical feedback. For that reason, consider asking, in addition to those with whom you are close, others who might not be friends— former teachers, coaches, mentors, supervisors you respect—but who might have a viewpoint or network you want to access.

At the same time, look beyond your immediate work context in selecting your advisers so that you have a board that will help you see your life in all its many dimensions. Most people are familiar with the notion of "360-degree" feedback. Companies use it to help employees learn from superiors, peers, and subordinates, in order to boost their performance and work-related interpersonal skills, and so forth. At New Directions, we have expanded that concept to include a broader range of noncareer inputs or angles, including our values, dreams, passions, even our spirituality. We call it "720-degree" feedback.

There is also an emotional component to having a board of advisers. In the process of transitions, we all experience frustrating moments or challenges that discourage us. We may be tempted to give up, to forget about trying to change. A board can give us the wherewithal to hang in there and continue. It's the beginning of a community that can sustain someone through transition.

How useful can this be? A client answered this by comparing a board of advisers to the friends who helped Uncle Wiggily, the gentlemen rabbit in the children's books by Howard R. Garis (1987). Often with a walking stick in one hand and valise in the other, "Uncle Wiggily was ready for any adventure because he was always networking," the client said, to my surprise. I went back and did some rereading. Sure enough, when the hero found himself in a bind, one or another member of his circle of forest friends would happen along to help him out. These helpers were small critters and forest folk who formed a sort of board of personal advisers to Uncle Wiggily. Not only did they help him, but also he often posed solutions that bailed them out of problems. What works for Uncle Wiggily works for people in transition. Aren't we all kids at heart?

The title of a different children's book describes one of two final points I want to make in this preview of creating a life portfolio. If you have read the Dr. Seuss book *Oh, the Places You'll Go!* (Seuss, 1990), you will know something about the portfolio process: it requires entering new networks and new arenas.

If one of your objectives is to throw open the window and explore broadly the range of possibilities that you might not otherwise be exposed to, then you are going to have to talk to new people. You are going to have to get into new situations and open up new territory. That's important. If you talk to the same people all the time, you are not going to learn much in terms of new opportunities. You have to reach beyond your current network.

My closing point is that the process is highly individual. One of the first things portfolio clients do when they come to New Directions is to create, along with their primary consultants, a specific, customized process unique to their individual needs, situation, experience, and personality. Our resources are tailored to those specifics. As a result, no two programs are alike.

On the other hand, all portfolios, at least with us, start with the importance of three elements: *weaning, a personal board of advisers,* and *the beginning of assessment,* all building toward a personal mission statement. The direction one ends up taking evolves from the discipline and integrity of these three building blocks.

Profiles in Portfolio

Older Americans who want a robust life portfolio of work, play, discovery, and purpose don't have to look far for inspiration. Any history book or even a good daily newspaper will do. Today, and throughout our history, remarkable men and women have lived vigorous, adaptable, meaningful lives into their very late years. No, they didn't call their sense of personal reinvention a *portfolio mind-set,* but that doesn't matter. They embodied the message of this book by staying active and vital as they aged, taking on new causes, and creating personal legacies—sometimes by a shift to a new direction.

Thomas Jefferson, I know, has other claims to fame, but he truly was a pioneer in seeing retirement as an opportunity. He retired in 1809 at age fifty-six after two terms as president. But instead of dreading life without the trappings of power, Jefferson said he looked forward to it "with the fondness of a sailor who has land in view." He pursued a cornucopia of activities in music, architecture, chemistry, farming, the study of religion, philosophy, law, and education. He experimented with new crops and farming techniques at Monticello and corresponded with persons all over the world. One of his most significant legacies was the founding of the University of Virginia, again something of a postcareer project, the fulfillment of a dream he had had for decades. Jefferson lobbied for its charter, secured its location, designed its buildings, devised its curriculum, hired the faculty, donated the books, and served as the university's first rector.

At the height of his career, **Andrew Carnegie,** who lived from 1835 to 1919, was second in wealth only to John D. Rockefeller. But the self-made steel magnate understood that even if you have all the money in the world, you need something engaging and valuable to do when work is done. After selling U.S. Steel to J. P. Morgan for $480 million at age sixty-five, Carnegie decided to launch a new career of philanthropy and service focused on education and literacy. "I have known millionaires starving for lack of that nutriment that sustains all that is human in man," he wrote. In his book, *Gospel of Wealth,* Carnegie urged the rich to use their wealth to help improve society. Carnegie loved books as a child, especially the works of Shakespeare. He saw the public library system as a way to share that love. He funded more than three thousand public libraries around the world, including at least one in almost every U.S. state. By the time he died at age eighty-three, he had given away almost $351 million (much of it going to the creation of schools and universities); upon his death, the last $30 million was donated to foundations and charities.

It is only a small exaggeration to say that during the nadir of World War II, it took a man past official retirement age, a political leader widely regarded as washed up, to rally and save the Western world. The man, of course, was **Winston Churchill.** As he progressed from war correspondent to member of Parliament early on, Churchill was often seen as erratic and undependable. A hero in the Boer War, he became First Lord of the Admiralty at age thirty-seven, but after a military blunder he was unjustly discredited and cashiered out of office. His political aspirations were in tatters. However, in 1940, at age sixty-six, Churchill became prime minister and displayed the leadership, inspiration, and unwavering devotion to victory for which the world remembers him. Churchill wrote later: "I felt as if I had been walking with destiny, and that all my past life had been but a preparation for this hour and for this trial" (1986, p. 667).

When he left that post in 1945, Churchill could have languished in the role of elder statesman. Instead, he created a diverse tableau of projects, interests, and activities, becoming an avid writer and landscape painter. Hearing the call, he also returned to the House of Commons, where he served as opposition leader. In 1951, he became prime minister a second time, at age seventy-six. When Churchill was seventy-nine, his six-volume *The Second World War* was awarded the Nobel Prize for Literature. When his second term as prime minister ended at age eighty-one, Churchill dedicated much of his time to painting, writing, and being with his family. His four-volume *A History of the English-Speaking Peoples* was published between 1956 and 1958, when he was well into his eighties. He died at age ninety.

(Continued)

Her husband may have helped invent modern retirement, but **Eleanor Roosevelt** was aware that Americans needed more than financial security to flourish as they aged. "If man is to be liberated to enjoy more leisure, he must also be prepared to enjoy this leisure fully and creatively," she wrote in her syndicated newspaper column "My Day," on November 5, 1958. "Let us begin to think how we can prepare old and young for these new opportunities." Roosevelt was the nation's First Lady for twelve years. When that role ended upon Franklin Roosevelt's death in 1945, she found new passions and resumed old ones. Her signature achievement was the key role she played in the creation of the Universal Declaration of Human Rights in 1948 and its adoption by the United Nations. She also continued to write and became one of the first women to participate in the sport of bow hunting and competitive archery. Roosevelt spoke out well into her seventies in support of numerous causes, including equal rights for women and efforts to eradicate poverty.

We may know **Harland David Sanders** as the "Colonel" of Kentucky Fried Chicken, but we may not know that he began that business at age sixty-seven. Before then, he worked as a firefighter, steamboat driver, insurance salesman, Army private, motel owner, and gas station owner. The legend is that when Sanders got his first Social Security check, he sank it into the beginnings of his fast-food enterprise. Sanders cooked at home after his father died and his mother went to work. And he always loved it. As a gas station owner, he sold chicken that he had made with a special blend of herbs and spices. People loved his "finger-lickin' good" chicken so much that Sanders decided to sell his recipe to restaurants. He traveled around Kentucky, often sleeping in his car, trying to convince restaurants to buy it. He was told no more than a thousand times. But he knew he had a good idea, so he decided to go it alone. Where did he summon the will to start his own business at that point in his life? It was not desire for money. "There's no reason to be the richest man in the cemetery," he once said. "You can't do any business from there." It was simply his love of his work that drove him on. Sanders sold Kentucky Fried Chicken in 1964, at age seventy-four, and remained its spokesman and public face for fifteen more years. He died at age ninety.

—Sarah McAdams Corbett

CHAPTER SIX

TIME TO GIVE BACK

Giving of our time and energy to help others is an integral part of creating and sustaining a successful life portfolio. There are many reasons for this. A key one is that during major work or life transitions, people need to connect with their core values and priorities. They also need to get a perspective on life, the proverbial view from ten thousand feet. How can we do this? We can, and I think should, reach out for help. We can also *give help to others.* I know this may not sound logical, but I am positive that it works. Giving back to others can generate amazing energy and progress in your life as you move forward into your newest chapter.

When Bob Williams, whom I quoted earlier, entered portfolio, he ramped up his involvement with several nonprofit groups. "These pro bono pieces are the *whole* anchor of portfolio," Bob told me not long ago. I agree.

Officially, we call this slice of the portfolio pie *humanitarian and community interests,* but informally we call it *giving back.* Why not simply giving? We could say that, but calling it giving *back* adds something important. To me, it suggests a sharing, a partnership, or even an exchange. We give back because we have been given so much. Giving back completes a circle.

How does it help us move forward when we begin a life change? People in transition need to maintain strong self-esteem. It has been my experience that those who give back regularly feel good about themselves. I remember a client who came to New Directions after losing his job at a bank. John, as I will call him, had a rough time. His job hunt went on longer than anticipated. He began to look discouraged when I saw him. After being out of work for two years, he decided to volunteer through a nonprofit we created, the Foundation for New Directions. At the New England Shelter for Homeless Veterans, he taught classes and coached the vets on how to find work; for example, advising them how to write a résumé or conduct themselves in an interview. He threw himself into it and did a great job.

The director of our foundation, Mary Westropp, was so impressed watching John run workshops for the veterans that she gave him an impromptu promotion. One day, John bounded into my office, exclaiming, "Mary calls me Professor!" All of a sudden, he had a title for himself: "Professor." And he began to look and talk the part. His new passion for volunteering helped restore his self-esteem and zest for life and that in turn helped him network better. In the end, the man who came back from feeling down landed a very good job.

LARGER PURPOSES

Giving back increases our awareness of and commitment to purposes bigger than we are. It can make us begin to think in terms of our legacies. Lacking purpose can set us adrift but so can failing to reexamine our purposes as our lives change. For many of us, the primary "reason for being" during most of adulthood is doing our jobs well. As we take on more financial obligations as our families grow and mature, this can become even more the case. We always know what we have to do—provide what is needed to keep everything running. Take the job away at fifty-five or sixty-five or seventy-five, and even the most balanced, upbeat, change-oriented individuals face a challenge in redefining their mission in life. The failure to meet this challenge has turned many a retirement into a prison of boredom.

British sociologist Paul Thompson confirmed this point in *I Don't Feel Old: The Experience of Later Life* (1990). His research found that a loss of purpose posed a bigger threat to the psychological well-being of aging Americans than a loss of income or money. Significantly, Thompson said his subjects reported that they "didn't feel old" as long as they had a sense of purpose from doing volunteer work, social relationships, grandparenting, creative hobbies, even religious beliefs.

Another important study of adults over age sixty-five showed that volunteering helps us live longer. In 1986, sociologists at the

University of Michigan began a longitudinal study of 1,210 adults. They wanted to know if giving back had measurable effects on mental and physical well-being. About 425 of the subjects (35 percent) said they volunteered at least forty hours per year at a church, charity, or other nonprofit group. The others did so either sporadically or not at all. After eight years, the data showed that—factoring in baseline variables in physical health, income, and social life—the individuals in the volunteering group lived longer.

Even more significant is what the study concluded about people who give time to a *single cause*. A subgroup within the volunteering adults said that they gave all their volunteer time to one charitable project or effort. After eight years, this subgroup had a 40 percent greater chance of being alive than the overall group of nonvolunteers. The subjects who volunteered regularly but spread their time among several organizations did not gain this advantage. One message is that a consistent habit of volunteering, rather than just doing it once or twice here and there, enhances our vitality and well-being. And when people believe in an activity or project enough to put all their volunteer time into it, which seems to define having a sense of purpose, the effect is magnified.

WIDER BENEFITS

Americans who give back add a lot of value to our society in many ways. One group, Independent Sector, has figured out that it would take nine million paid employees working full time to replace the work done each year by volunteers. Unfortunately, the social needs they address are growing. Almost every day, newspapers confirm how economically divided our society is. Markets for luxury goods and services are flourishing, while an estimated thirteen million children in America lack proper nutrition. More people make more money than they really need, yet more people are not making as much as they do need.

A survey by market research firm TNS Financial Services found that American households with a net worth of $1 million or more last year rose by 700,000, or 8 percent, over 2004. The number of such households totals 8.9 million, says TNS. Conversely, 37 million Americans were living in poverty in 2004, according to government statistics, and 45 million lacked health insurance. In the period from 2000 to 2004, the ranks of the poor increased by 5.5 million. Ronald Reagan was right when he said, "The government declared war on poverty. Poverty won."

These jarring contrasts are why giving back after our primary careers recede is a win-win proposition. It provides help that America needs desperately to address these gaps. But the plain truth is that giving back also enriches our lives. There is a "return" on our investment of time. I truly believe that this is not selfish, a what's-in-it-for-me way of thinking, or it should not be. Rather, it is a clear and bold statement of an ageless truth.

"If you spend yourselves in behalf of the hungry and satisfy the needs of the oppressed, then your light will rise in the darkness," the prophet Isaiah says in the Hebrew Bible (*NRSV,* Isaiah 58:10). "The Lord will guide you always; he will satisfy your needs . . . and will strengthen your frame. You will be like a well-watered garden, like a spring whose waters never fail." Ralph Waldo Emerson also expressed this wisdom when he observed that the laws of the universe are such that those who give time, money, or shelter to strangers practically "put God under obligation" to them. "In some way the time they seem to lose is redeemed, and the pains they seem to take remunerate themselves" (1983, p. 369).

I am sometimes surprised that more people are not aware that givers are getters. Why? Volunteering gets you out of your own skin, helps you develop new contacts and friendships. You are using your intellect, teaching skills, leadership experience, or tapping into your empathy and compassion. All of these are valued and put to good use. You network better because you feel more "up" about yourself and about life in general.

Empirical data supports this view. Highly organized social activity, such as regular volunteering, "is the single strongest predictor, other than smoking, of longevity and vitality," according to two social scientists, Jean Grossman and Kathryn Furano. Volunteering predicts higher psychological well-being, lower depression, and better self-reported physical health in later midlife. "Everything we know," according to another researcher, UCLA psychiatrist Arnold Scheibel, "indicates that being busy, having a sense of commitment, a sense of being something other than passive and useless is very positive for health."

Getting from Giving

Ruth Roberson was eighty-one when she lost her last family member. She was living in Las Vegas, where she ran the dress department at a local store, and cared for her learning-disabled adult daughter, Susan. Ruth was from North Carolina and had lived there most of her life. But when her husband died at age sixty-two in 1973, she and Susan moved to Nevada. In 2001, Susan died at age forty-seven. Ruth brought her body back to be buried in the family plot in Greensboro and stayed.

Alone, Ruth said she began to feel that there was nothing to look forward to. She visited her daughter's grave a lot. "The doctor said I was spending too much time at the cemetery," Ruth recalled. "But I was grieving. I'd lost all I had." In 2002, Ruth saw an ad for a caregiver for Home Instead Senior Care, a national provider of nonmedical home care for seniors. It didn't pay much, but being a caregiver appealed to her. Ruth called and was hired. She began caring for four people—a woman and her autistic son and a couple in their early nineties—thirty-eight hours per week.

Home Instead named Ruth its Caregiver of the Year in North Carolina three years ago. Today, Ruth, who is eighty-five, says her work has given her a new lease on life.

"It's so fulfilling," she said. "On Saturday and Sunday, I can't wait for Monday to get here, so I can be with people. I try to do my best. The doctor says, 'Whatever you're doing, just keep on doing it—because you're the healthiest woman I've ever seen.'" Ruth says events have borne out what she said when she interviewed for the job. "I told him whoever they would give me to help would help me even more."

Even donating money to others confers benefits, Arthur C. Brooks, an economics professor at Syracuse University wrote in an opinion column in the *Wall Street Journal* (December 8, 2005). "The evidence is unambiguous that donating money (and time) is one of the best ways to buy happiness," wrote Brooks. He said that people who donate to charity are 40 percent more likely than nondonors to say they are very happy with their lives.

OUR OWN EFFORT

The Foundation for New Directions confirms that giving back is a win-win. A registered nonprofit organization, it taps clients to provide job coaching to homeless veterans, inner-city youth, and other low-income job trainees. The mentors are senior executives and professionals who themselves may be looking for a new job.

Westropp, the director, says that as a group, the volunteers are among the most exuberant people she knows. In putting their focus on others in need, the volunteers reactivate a sense of their own expertise and enjoy the exhilaration of helping others change their lives.

I started the foundation when I became troubled that many people could not afford the services to help them find meaningful work. I knew that our clients could provide valuable help to others in a tough situation, but I also felt that the experience would benefit our clients. At first, we experimented with placing our clients with other nonprofit agencies but quickly realized that we needed a formal, recognizable infrastructure.

I talked to many people, including colleagues. We came up with the 501C3 for the project and launched. A mainstay organization has been the New England Shelter for Homeless Veterans. Our clients march from the waterfront up to 17 Court Street in Boston, where the shelter is located, roll up their sleeves, and give these guys and women a ton of TLC and top-level guidance. A lot of heroic effort goes on behind the scenes to make it happen.

I am proud to say that so many clients have been job mentors to well over nine hundred individuals in need since we started in 1996. It has been gratifying to watch that but also to see and listen to the people they help. So many of them show so much heart in their struggle to change their lives.

For our clients, the positive effects have been nothing short of incredible. It enhances their self-image and willingness to meet new people. And it gives them a sometimes much-needed change in perspective. It has been a way for people to meet the developmental psychological needs that emerge in late middle age, the period that psychologist Erik Erikson called the *generativity stage.* It's about the growing capacity to care and desire to give to others.

Will Boomers Reinvent Volunteering?

Concern has arisen about whether the Baby Boom generation will step up to meet the country's need for volunteers in the nonprofit sector. The Harvard School of Public Health and MetLife Foundation issued a report in 2004, "Reinventing Aging," which warned that boomers are not joiners and had historically low rates of civic involvement. The report suggested that boomers might disappoint hopes that they will volunteer their time.

But the Harvard report focused on potential disconnects between boomer lifestyles and expectations and the styles or cultures of traditional charities and service organizations. However, plenty of evidence indicates that boomers do want purposeful work in their fifties, sixties, and seventies. At the end of 2005, the Bureau of Labor Statistics announced that baby boomers have the highest volunteer rate of any demographic group. Nearly one-third of them volunteer in a variety of capacities. Interestingly, boomers who work are the most involved in giving back.

Those numbers will only grow. The Corporation for National and Community Service has begun a "Get Involved" campaign targeted at boomers. The group argues that boomers—many of whom came of age during the presidency of John F. Kennedy—are idealists and want to make a difference.

The 2005 Merrill Lynch New Retirement Survey revealed that ten times as many boomer respondents said they "put others first" as said "put themselves first"; as the study organizers said, "The me generation has grown up to be a *we* generation." And a Civic Ventures poll, reported in its 2005 *New Face of Work Survey* (MetLife Foundation and Civic Ventures, 2005), found that 57 percent of people over age fifty want work in retirement that gives them a sense of purpose and benefits other people.

This lines up with our experience at New Directions, where the majority of portfolio clients choose to spend at least part of their time giving back.

(Continued)

The Harvard-MetLife study, "Reinventing Aging," did highlight an important issue: that boomers want to volunteer on their
own terms (for starters, they don't like the term *volunteering*).
To draw them in, the nonprofit world may have to adjust its
"interface" with potential volunteers. Here are some thoughts
they should consider:

Boomers want flexibility in volunteer placements and
might respond better to more informal and short-term volunteer assignments that they select.

Boomers don't want to waste their time on a volunteer
placement at an organization they perceive to be disorganized
or poorly run. Volunteering, rather than being a replacement
for leisure time, will be a continuation of work for boomers.
So they'll choose nonprofit organizations with the same gravity
they would use to select an employer.

Using *paid volunteers,* who receive at least a stipend for
their time, is increasingly popular. The organization ReServe:
Next Steps for Older Adults, for example, connects older
adults to stipend-paying opportunities at nonprofits.

Boomers want to feel that they are not just making sand-
wiches but making a significant difference—and they want to
use their skills and experience to do it. *Fortune* magazine pro-
filed a woman who illustrates the frustration of older adults
who want to use their talents for more than volunteer busy-
work. A professor of medicine, she signed up to volunteer in
a Florida hospital after retiring, only to be given the role of
refilling water pitchers. (The story was entitled "Candy Striper,
My Ass!") One solution is that nonprofits ask managers and
professionals to donate managerial skills at a high level on an
as-needed basis.

A 2005 report released by the Center for Corporate Citi-
zenship at Boston College and Volunteers of America suggests
that nonprofits work with companies to develop the "volunteer
DNA" of their boomer employees long before they retire, offering service opportunities early on so they get hooked and continue after moving on.

TAKING THE CALL

After Hurricane Katrina struck in 2005, the foundation asked clients to pitch in. Private managerial skills, compassion, and, frankly, muscle were needed to run a large shelter for displaced hurricane victims at a Massachusetts military base. One of the calls went to Betsy Seeley, a client and previous volunteer who lives in a suburb of Boston. Knowing she could be of help—Betsy had made systems work as an operations manager in financial services and health care—she didn't dawdle. She agreed to be the shelter's chief of staff, even though it meant a 150-plus mile commute two or three days a week.

After she hung up, Betsy said her fifteen-year-old daughter asked why she had agreed to such a time-consuming demand in late summer, when, in a few weeks, the daughter would be back in school. "I told her that these were folks who had lost everything and were in serious need," she said. "And I said that there are things in life you can't predict. When you get a call like that, you step up and you take it."

There was something else Betsy could not have known. Her five-week stint helped her land a job, as the interim operations chief for a large new arts center in the Boston area. Her interviewers later disclosed that the volunteer assignment at the shelter was the proverbial feather in her cap that proved she could transfer her operational skills to the nonprofit sector.

"When first I said yes, it was a gut response," Betsy said. "But from the point of view of my being in a job search, I realized fairly quickly that it was a way to stay in the game, especially since I wanted to work for a nonprofit."

A HABIT OF MIND

All of us have a tendency to dwell on our problems—the slights and resentments of our lives, the things that failed or never came to pass. Seeing the needs of other people and helping them address those needs often reminds us that we have far more to be thankful for. For those who have been given much, and I include myself, giving back simply feels like a right and good response.

But I urge people to think about any expectations they have for their humanitarian, community-based, or nonprofit involvements. Like networking, volunteering should not be done to achieve an end (whether personal fulfillment or tax break) or broader social goal (change the world). Rather, it should be done as what the short story writer Flannery O'Connor calls a *habit of mind*, a routine, an integrated part of how you see the world and what you do.

The demographic phenomenon—more healthy, wealthy, and better-educated older Americans than ever before in our history— is a unique opportunity in our country. We should do everything we can as a society to leverage the experience, knowledge, and skills of this group for the public good. Unfortunately, it is still too hard for older Americans to find socially useful work, whether it be paid or unpaid. This gap in our response to changing demographics, and the possible benefits for everyone if we closed it, are discussed in the next chapter.

CHAPTER SEVEN

CLOSING THE GAP

Evelyn Ostergren of San Francisco was the office manager of a nonprofit organization. At sixty-three, she wasn't ready to retire, but she didn't want to keep doing the same thing. "I'm luckier than many people my age, but I have the same questions," she said. "What am I? A senior citizen? An elder? A golden ager? They don't fit, but there's no good word for this twenty-year period of life I'm in. How will I decide what I want? Who do I turn to for advice, ideas, encouragement?"

At age sixty-two and a half, Ostergren became old enough under present law for partial Social Security payments. Crossing that age threshold can be a disorienting experience. Many people have the odd feeling that the social expectations that go along with the dubious honor of being a "senior citizen" must apply to *someone else.*

On balance, they tend to feel the same as ever—no less interested in life, no less able to contribute, no less vital. And indeed many people their age and older are still in the thick of it. They run entertainment conglomerates (for example, Rupert Murdoch, seventy-five, and Sumner Redstone, eighty-two), investment companies (for example, Warren Buffett, seventy-five), and the Federal Reserve (for example, Alan Greenspan before he retired at seventy-nine). Architect Frank Gehry designs world-class buildings at age seventy-seven. At seventy-eight, Joe Paterno coaches the Penn State football team. Others seek quieter ways to contribute and give back.

But at the supermarket or movie theater, on a train or in a restaurant, they are asked if they qualify for the senior discount or if they want the early-bird senior special. Are you a *senior citizen,* the clerk wants to know? There is nothing wrong with such questions, and everyone loves a discount. The problem is that "senior citizens" have changed, but the social response to them has not kept pace.

That musty label reminds older Americans of the lack of resources, guidance, and support from society in writing the next chapter of their lives. Workplaces and our social institutions have generally lagged in their response to the alteration of the life span. Experts call this a *structural gap* between what is and what should be.

Again, Freedman of Civic Ventures has said it well. "We do a much better job helping people plan financially for the second half of life," he wrote in a summary of Civic Ventures' 2005 *New Face of Work Survey,* "than we do helping them navigate their way from one phase of life and work to engagement in another." (Freedman's essay, "The Boomers, Good Work, and the Next Stage of Life," can be found at www.civicventures.org/publications/surveys/new_ face_of_work/nfw_essay.pdf.) I believe that using some innovative thinking and entrepreneurial drive to close this gap carries multiple potential benefits.

• Individuals navigating this terrain would get support, resources, and encouragement to seek out creative alternatives to retirement. Options or opportunities that would not otherwise exist would be open to them.

• Businesses would benefit from responding to new workplace realities and workers' new expectations and preferences. The old college-career-retirement model of employment no longer serves. Companies that don't adapt may not stay in business.

• The country would benefit if we could apply the energy, experience, and talent of older people to those who need help the most. We waste opportunities to put their capital to work in education, health care, social services, and other fields. As C. Eugene Steuerle of the Urban Institute said before a congressional panel last year, "People in their late fifties, sixties, and seventies have now become the largest underutilized pool of human resources in the economy."

We can and must expand the range of choices we offer older Americans. Indeed, we should for all ages. There is no reason why

"Are you sure this ice floe is going to pass by the nursing home?"

we cannot respond better to older Americans' desire to do good work—but to do it in ways that give them choice and flexibility.

Consider this: more than thirty million Americans will attain traditional retirement age over the next fifteen years, creating turnover in many fields and industries. And the current view is that four out of five of these people expect to work past that point. That is the *supply* side of the equation. Now let's look at the *demand* side: some two-thirds of U.S. employers don't actively recruit older workers! Most companies don't even do well at *retaining* key senior employees.

The most frequently reported preferences of working adults these days are for flexibility in work arrangements, individual choice in work agendas, and ways to balance work and life. A 2005 survey by AARP, the membership group for older Americans, found that almost two in five workers expressed interest in phased retirement, and more than half said they would like to trim their weekly work schedule by twelve hours. But only one company in five offers flexible work arrangements, sabbaticals, and learning programs that would meet this need.

Much needs to be done. Companies will have to become more creative and flexible in planning for the anticipated wave of retirements. In public policy, we have to remove obstacles that block employers from hiring older workers, in particular the high cost of providing health coverage for them. As a nation, we have to do more than give creative alternatives to retirement more visibility and acceptance. Let's sell people on those alternatives. I agree with David Ellis, whom I mentioned earlier. "Thought leaders in business, education, and government have to be forceful about naming the new realities that make retirement more likely at eighty than sixty. We have to teach it and preach it."

Everywhere we have to get rid of the outdated rules, practices, and ways of thinking that continue to retire people prematurely. What thinking do I mean? Lee Iacocca said it well.

"I've always been against automated, chronological dates to farm people out," the former Chrysler chief and corporate guru recently said. "The union would always say, 'Make room for the new blood; there aren't enough jobs to go around.' Well, what a policy to have. I have people at Chrysler who were forty but acted eighty, and I have eighty-year-olds who could do everything a forty-year-old could do. You have to take a different view of age now. People are living longer. Age just gives experience. Besides, it takes you until fifty to know what the hell is going on in the world."

But we should accept the reality that corporations and institutions may not do very much to help people create life portfolios, or certainly not very soon. So individuals have to step up to the plate. It is they and their families who lead the way and corporations and programs that will follow.

That means that "seeing what is out there" for you is probably not enough. Instead, know what you can do that is of value in the world, then go out and create a need for it. And let us encourage young people to anticipate and assume the portfolio mind-set. Spread the word: don't just think career trajectory. Think larger life plan.

AN OPPORTUNITY FOR BUSINESS

Corporate America was served well by the notion of a linear career and has resisted its replacement—the notion that most hold a portfolio of jobs over the course of their lives. But now it will have to accommodate portfolio thinking in how employment is structured. Companies must offer flexible or phased retirement options, recognize the value of sabbaticals and lateral career moves within a company, and redeploy older workers more skillfully.

If there is a new social contract implicit between employers and employees today, it should be this: you give me your labor, and I guarantee that as long as you work here and perform, I will give you every opportunity to become more employable, more versatile, and more engaged, such that you will never retire.

Ideas like these may be threatening. But companies that don't change their thinking will see their skills, knowledge capital, and their hope of future leadership drain away. In *The Perfect Labor Storm Fact Book* (2004), Ira S. Wolfe reports that, as we noted earlier, one out of five Fortune 500 companies will be losing 40 percent of its management over the next five years. Yet most CEOs readily admit that their companies do not have a formal leadership succession plan and are not planning adequately for the coming wave of retirements.

One innovative approach that deserves to be mentioned as a positive example is that of Europe's second-largest papermaker. The Finnish company UPM was concerned that few young people wanted to take jobs left open by older workers, who often retired as soon as they were eligible, at around age sixty. As some older workers neared retirement, they also displayed a waiting-for-the-gold-watch outlook that hurt productivity. How could they motivate them to stay on the job rather than retire? UPM began annual off-site conferences for mill hands in their forties and fifties. In addition to relaxing, they learned about the company's flexible work and job retraining options and about maintaining fitness and health. They were also treated as valuable sources of ideas about UPM's operations and future. Many of the reengaged older workers took new interest and pride in their jobs and elected to postpone retirement. Older workers as a group began to take the least sick days of all employees.

Flexible or phased retirement is not a perfect solution, but it is a good start. Take MITRE Corporation, a technology research and development company in Bedford, Massachusetts. Its older engineers' deep technical knowledge in certain older fields important to the company, including radar, was in danger of being lost. To keep its competitive edge, MITRE created a *reserve team* of retirees who come back to work on short-term projects. It permits workers to slowly wean into retirement by working fewer hours, or days, per week.

YourEncore, of Indianapolis, Indiana, is taking that idea to another level. It helps companies locate and hire retired workers for projects. It's the brainchild of three companies, Procter and Gamble, Eli Lilly, and Boeing. Each of them was separately concerned about losing top talent and wanted a way to tap into the expertise of their many retirees. They formed a network of retired scientists and engineers that any of them could use to solve problems or generate ideas.

That network turned into YourEncore. Companies belonging to the YourEncore network can tap into its pool of 925 *experts,* as it calls its retired workers for hire. Projects typically last six to eight weeks at a pace of twenty to thirty hours a week. Brad Lawson, who heads YourEncore, said that the companies love the idea, noting that 90 percent of the projects finish ahead of schedule and under budget. "It's like getting the enthusiasm and passion of a new hire with the wisdom and experience of a proven veteran."

The workers, Lawson said, "wanted to leave the workforce for personal pursuits, and yet they want to get back into the workforce—just not at twelve hours a day," he said. The projects help them stay connected and vital, he added. At the same time, "They like doing these projects because they know there's a beginning and an end."

Short-term or bridge jobs do fill a social need, but I should caution that they are not well suited, in the end, to true portfolio lifestyle. People in portfolio need more than scattered or tentative activities that cannot be sustained over time. The ideal thing is to have pursuits, activities, and commitments that provide a sense of "glue" to one's life—not those that arise or disappear at the whim of institutions or corporations. We come back to the fact that in portfolio, it is the individuals who are CEOs of their own lives.

One company staring the challenge of managerial succession in the face is Fidelity Investments. The result has been innovative approaches that benefit all involved. "This is a chance for companies to step up and be more creative and flexible," said Ellen Wilson, executive vice president of human resources at the financial services giant. Fidelity has forty thousand employees. "We looked at how many of our employees will be fifty-plus over the next five to ten years, to determine what our needs are. We don't have all the answers, but we *do* know that we cannot let this intellectual capital leave us."

Wilson said that Fidelity has made it "culturally acceptable to raise your hand and say you're thinking about retirement." When managers do that, the company begins talking informally with them about possible variations. "In each business unit, we've tried to find ways for individuals to let us know whether they might be interested in staying on, perhaps part-time, in a role where they can add value and be a resource to the next generation of leaders, but without impeding them." Wilson added that the company's executives have been receptive to continuing to contribute.

Opportunities for retired Fidelity employees include mentoring younger managers and analysts and helping new employees navigate the company. They can also represent the company in working personally with individual clients, marketing, philanthropic activities, community, and government relations. In addition, Wilson added, they are welcome to be consultants on special projects, acquisition activity, and strategic investments.

"We don't want to create a program," she said. "This has to be at the discretion of management. But you need solid input, so there's a lot of need for conversation." For that to work, "you have to have a real relationship with your people, a level of *trust* in your system."

Here are some additional ideas companies should consider:

- *Lifelong learning.* Companies should be encouraged with tax incentives to offer in-house learning opportunities. The more of these they provide, the more they widen the skill base of their workforce and fulfill a moral obligation to workers whose jobs might not be secure. An interest in learning new things helps individuals embrace change as normal. United Technology Corporation has been innovative here. Its pays 100 percent of the costs for employees who go back to school. Students can obtain a degree in any field, whether or not it is related to their jobs, and are allowed up to three hours a week of paid time off for studying. Those who receive a degree are rewarded with a number of shares of UTC common stock, depending on the degree.
- *Sabbaticals.* Surveys show that despite the proven benefits, relatively few companies offer them. Employees should be given time to pursue special projects or research, rest, invest in their families,

and come back recharged. Watson Wyatt Worldwide, a human resources consulting firm, reports that "companies find if they don't offer sabbaticals, their executives will burn out and leave— or worse, they'll burn out and stay."

• *Redeployment.* Increase awareness of the benefits of redeploying key people. Create new internal job responsibilities, revise old ones, rearrange the division of responsibilities. Turn your managers and administrators to "faculty" members at your company.

POLICY OBSTACLES

The government also has work to do. There remain too many barriers to flexible employment arrangements and longer work for older workers in our laws, regulations, and policies. Labor regulations are stuck in the days when full-time work led only to full-time retirement. According to a study by the Employment Policy Foundation, 65 percent of employers would offer phased-in retirement but say government regulations keep them from doing so.

Some government efforts are moving forward. One example came in 2000, when Uncle Sam stopped penalizing Americans who continue to work after age sixty-five by denying them Social Security benefits. The IRS now lets people fifty-nine and a half or older receive partial payments even while they continue working. If people are not forced to retire to get a pension, they are more likely to stay on the job.

But changes are needed in regulations governing defined benefit pensions. Under most plans, payments are set according to rate of pay in the last few years of work. That discourages workers from pursuing flexible retirement options (without officially retiring and taking a pension) because it would reduce their hours and pay, thereby reducing their eventual pension payments.

A bigger challenge is realigning our federal Social Security program to the reality of our longer lives. Social Security was conceived as a supplement to the savings of older Americans. Today it is a safety net for more than ten million people, who live on that check alone, according to the government. To make sure the program is there for those who most need it, it makes sense to raise the full retirement age to seventy and increase the age at which people can draw early partial payments. (Flexibility would have to

Opportunities for Older Individuals

Coming to realize that you are not living the life you always imagined for yourself? The good news is that you have plenty of time to try something new—and fields to tap into. Industries including health care, education, social services, retail, technology, manufacturing, utilities, and construction anticipate a serious labor shortage over the next twenty years. And older workers are in demand. Surveys by the Bureau of Labor Statistics showed that workers age fifty-five and older found new jobs faster in 2005 than younger folks.

But also remember that work opportunities are not limited to existing fields, industries, and companies. We may be entering a golden age for the small entrepreneur, according to Thomas Malone, a professor at MIT's Sloan School of Management. Malone thinks the Internet and powerful new off-the-shelf communications technologies have created an environment in which one out of ten new small businesses (employing from one to ten people) can succeed. Additional questions to ask:

- *Do you have experience in health care?* Americans over age sixty-five account for half of physician visits and half of all hospital stays, and health services will be strained by the aging of the Baby Boom generation. The result is a shortage of physicians, physician assistants, nurses, physical therapists, home care workers, dental hygienists, and even ambulance drivers.
- *Always wanted to teach?* Student enrollment is rising in all levels, but teachers continue to leave the profession. Already, more than 25 percent of U.S. teachers are at least fifty years old, and the median age is forty-four. Experts predict that over the next ten years, the nation will need as many as 2.4 million teachers.
- *Interested in designing new community spaces?* Opportunities exist in the planning and design of longevity-oriented communities. Some will serve elders with special interests, such as in health and fitness or art and culture. There is also a demand to design and build university-based intergenerational housing.

(Continued)

- *Good with people?* Consider the retail world. According to federal figures, worker shortages in the retail sector are making it one of the fast-growing industries for job growth. Many large companies—Borders and Home Depot, for instance—are already recognizing the value of older workers' "people skills" and recruiting them in large numbers.
- *Want to give back?* Charitable organizations need accountable, well-educated, and experienced employees. Opportunities in that sector may hold jobs that combine income with a sense of doing meaningful work.
- *Can you think on paper?* If you are a skilled writer, consider a freelance commercial writing career. It can offer a flexible lifestyle, and in corporate communications it can pay up to $150 per hour.
- *Interested in career coaching?* Services that help people navigate their postcareer years will be in demand. One growth area is in developing for-hire teams of elders with various problem-solving talents, who are deployed to fix difficult community or business issues.
- *Love animals?* People are spending more and more time and money on their dogs. Any service that caters to this market, such as dog grooming, doggie day care, dog training, and high-end dog accessories, has growth potential.

For additional help, visit the Small Business Administration at www.sbaonline.sba.gov (tips on writing a business plan), the Service Corps of Retired Executives at www.score.org (business start-up case studies), and the *Wall Street Journal*'s Center for Entrepreneurs at www.startupjournal.com (success stories and business ideas).

be built in for people who want to stop doing physically challenging work or who are ill but would not qualify for disability insurance.) People will resist such a change, but how shocking can this be when I can look out my office window any day and see eighty-year-olds jogging along city streets?

What else could government do? Respondents to Civic Ventures' 2005 *New Face of Work Survey* strongly endorsed the idea that the government should take additional steps to promote volunteerism in the portfolio stage of life. Of a thousand people polled, 60 percent supported a tax credit for older Americans who volunteer in schools or social services, and 48 percent supported increasing funding for Americans who go back to school or get training to prepare for work in schools or social services.

One idea that deserves thought is reducing the link between salary and seniority. Perhaps we need to promote the notion that what matters is the intrinsic value of the work—and not how many years someone has been doing it. Isn't how much and how well a person works a better basis for valuation and compensation than time served?

A *New York Times* columnist argued that case last year. "Older workers are retiring before they are ready, getting 'free time' even though they're living longer, forcing younger people to work harder to support them," John Tierney wrote on June 21, 2005. Could this time be redistributed, he asked, "so that young people, like harried parents, could enjoy it instead of waiting to get it all as one lump sum?"

COMMUNITY SERVICE INITIATIVES

One hopeful sign comes from the opportunities growing in the realm of public service, through both national and community-based programs.

When Experience Corps began as a pilot project in five cities in 1995, it was the only such national project. It recruited retired men and women over age fifty-five to work in elementary schools. Today there are many such programs, and they deserve our support. Senior Corps is a clearinghouse for recruiting volunteers over age fifty-five, and so far it has linked more than five hundred thousand Americans to projects in education, the environment, and public safety. One of its big efforts is a foster grandparent program. Other programs include Volunteers in Medicine, in which physicians provide services to people without health insurance, and Troops to Teachers, which recruits retired military personnel to assist in public schools.

Initiatives should also come from the local level. Communities could learn from Chandler, Arizona, which has what it calls a *Boomerang* program for retired residents. The program's Web site provides links to local resources on lifelong learning, volunteering, second careers, and wellness programs.

And communities should also develop intergenerational programs and initiatives, putting old and young side by side. Studies have found that young people in such programs show measurable improvement in school attendance and in attitudes toward school and future attitudes toward elders. Older volunteers report benefits to themselves and the satisfaction of feeling useful and giving back.

One potentially promising idea we had was setting up volunteer advisory councils in areas with significant numbers of retirees. One or two times a year, the leaders of distant nonprofit organizations would travel to these communities. These councils could be called *mentoring centers*, because they could bring together retirees with vast strategic and other business skills and the nonprofits needing their help. This concept seems worth pursuing. So many retired people live in gated communities without enough to do. Let's not sit around and complain. Let's bring give-back opportunities to the gates. I'll bet hotel owners and airlines would contribute to transporting and housing these leaders during their visits to the mentoring centers.

The best thing about public service is that inspired individuals can make a difference. Just look at what Jack Hexter did. If he had had his way, Hexter would not have retired in 1978 from his tenured job as a history professor at Yale University. But the college's mandatory retirement age of sixty-five gave him no choice. (Yale has since dropped it.) Not ready to stop working, Hexter took a job teaching at Washington University in St. Louis, Missouri, where he remained for eleven years. After he left that position in 1990, at age eighty, he took up a new cause that defined the remainder of his life.

The Gulf War under the first President Bush ended in 1991. Hexter realized that thousands of soldiers, many of whom were in their forties and fifties, were poised to retire as the conflict wound down. Hexter saw a trove of talent and experience that could be tapped to teach children in our nation's poor schools. He knew it was a good idea, and a passion was conceived. Hexter spent years trying to persuade Congress to fund a Troops to Teachers law and eventually succeeded.

In 1994, Congress created and funded $65 million toward a program to turn retired veterans into teachers in poor school districts. In its first four years, Troops to Teachers placed more than three thousand ex-soldiers in teaching positions, and they say they are very likely to remain teachers for some time.

When Hexter died at eighty-six, in December 1996, Stanford University President Richard W. Lyman wrote, in a letter to the editor published in the *New York Times,* that he had "never seen a more dramatic example of what a single individual can accomplish . . . armed only with a good idea and boundless determination to see it put into effect."

AHEAD OF THE CURVE ON CAMPUS

Universities and colleges are leaders in rethinking attitudes and challenging traditional thinking about retirement, frequently offering faculty members the option to retire in phases, or to retire but then be rehired to teach part-time, do research, or take on special administrative roles. More than three hundred U.S. colleges and universities have also established *learning in retirement* programs that encourage alumni to audit classes, attend lectures and conferences, and go on expeditions with faculty members.

The Massachusetts Institute of Technology has set an admirable model with its Transitions at Work program, which invigorates older employees by helping them pursue new paths on the job. MIT's retention rate for workers over fifty is high, with one-third of its workforce fitting in that category, and it is the only university to be repeatedly cited by AARP as one the nation's best employers for workers over fifty. After talking with older workers to find out what would keep them from retiring, human resources administrators at MIT created two courses, "Shifting Gears" and "Managing Across Generations," which are open to anyone in the university system. The Transitions at Work program offers older workers retraining and development opportunities, career counseling, and scholarships to study new areas. It also offers retirement financial planning and flexible work options, including phased retirement.

We need to do what is necessary to speed up our society's adaptation to new opportunities and needs presented by extended middle age. But we cannot *wait* for things to get better. Individuals are more fleet of foot than institutions. So act entrepreneurially, if only to examine and change your own attitudes. When it comes to work, banish the attitude, "Who are you with?" and replace it with "What are you doing?" I had lunch awhile ago with a man who is a former professor at a major business school. I presented some of the questions and ideas I have discussed in this chapter. I expected a long lecture of a reply, I guess, so I was surprised when he boiled down the main solution to a few words: "Make yourself wanted and needed."

You will be better able to do that if you maintain an awareness of your life portfolio as a constant theme in the background of your life. From the very start, integrate your career with your larger life goals, your values, and your family. Train yourself to periodically look at what you are doing now in your life against the bigger picture. Know what you have to offer. If you do, you will be ahead of the curve all the way. When you leave a position, or a position leaves you, you will never have to go back to square one, because you will have been working on your goals all the way along.

"My central concern is encouraging people to seek, to experience, to plan, to create, and to dream," said William Copperthwaite, teacher, philosopher, and craftsman. "If enough people do this, we will find a better way."

One more thing. Tell your kids and friends and neighbors about your struggle. They will empathize, but more important, they will recognize that adjustments are required all the way through life. They may even assimilate, if only subconsciously, the need for planning to be prepared for change. In some ways, this is good news. We can be role models. We can model the portfolio mind-set, and those we love, in particular our children, can learn from us.

CHAPTER EIGHT

LISTEN TO YOUR LIFE

A solid process of self-discovery is the foundation of the portfolio alternative to retirement. We call this step assessment, and it's a large part of what we do at New Directions, because little forward motion occurs in the transition to portfolio without the regrounding and refocusing it offers. Assessment can help us reclaim who we are and set new paths and priorities for the remainder of our lives.

In assessment, we explore our human purposes and passions. As we do this, we ask questions: What energizes and calls us, now, at this point in our lives? What motivates us? What gets us up on Monday mornings? When do we feel most alive? Assessment is ultimately about being alert to clues that will help us take future steps. But it is enhanced by clues from the past. A lot of what we do is help people reclaim old visions—or plumb messages hidden or ignored in years gone by. Assessment does not change the messages. It helps us reinterpret them. What unrealized hopes or unfinished personal business do we carry inside? If these were worthwhile, what blocked us? Resolving these questions can lead to new attitudes, behaviors, and plans for action.

The focus is on skills and on our *intrinsic* assets—the wisdom, knowledge, and strongly held values and beliefs that underlie our skills and gifts. Such qualities take time and effort to fully explore. They may exist below the surface. They may have developed as a result of relatively recent work, interests, or other life experiences, but they may have originated in earlier experiences. In assessment, we try to raise these to a conscious level. Doing so reawakens who we really are and helps us set new paths.

Intrinsic qualities may not have labels or match job titles and responsibilities. To identify them, we have to know the truth about ourselves. But everybody has them. That is why we take to heart what Martin Buber said about our most important task in life, and it bears repeating: "Every person born in this world represents something new, something that never existed before, something original and unique," he wrote. "And every man's foremost task is the actualization of his unique, unprecedented and never-recurring possibilities" (1960, pp. 12–13).

This is a lifelong process, which is why I believe so strongly that assessment should be ageless. Personal stocktaking should be more frequent and routine than it is for all of us. We go to the doctor for a checkup each year. Doesn't it make sense to have at least a biannual reality check about our personal and professional hopes and dreams? Probe what abilities we may have that we are not using? Most of us update our investment portfolios or meet with a financial planner to review our situations. We do so in part because investment opportunities and financial needs change. Doesn't it make sense that our motivations and goals also change?

On the other hand, it is true that people who have done well in their careers, raised families, and met financial goals are also good candidates for assessment. They tend to have acquired a pretty good knowledge of their strengths and weaknesses, what makes them happy or sad, thrilled or disappointed, empathetic or angry. Along with this self-knowledge comes a growing desire to reflect, to see the figure in the fabric of our lives. It becomes more natural to make a mental inventory of accomplishments and disappointments, contributions and relationships.

There is sadness in this, for we are up against limits. We are mortal human beings. But there is excitement, too. People in late middle age more than ever can imagine an active and significant personal future. Portfolio can be a time when your confirmed gifts find their fullest expression, when you go back to school, retrain for a new profession, launch a business, get serious about community service, or do some combination of these. Maturity gives a deeper tone and character to the search for self-fulfillment. We learn to see life through less of an economic lens. We may be drawn to spend more time with children and grandchildren, volunteer, work on causes dear to us, and develop ourselves spiritually.

NOT EVEN KNOWING THE QUESTIONS

Assessment can be a challenge for people who made the mistake, as many of us have, of letting ourselves be defined only by our careers. This may work for a while, especially when we are younger, but we must broaden our sense of ourselves to attain the greatest happiness. I have worked with many clients who had discovered, as one client told me, "When I surrendered my title, I surrendered my identity." I remember the senior partner of a law firm who at age sixty decided to move into portfolio rather than remaining on board as his firm merged with another one. He used a striking real estate metaphor to describe how he had given over his consciousness to his job: "Being a rainmaker is no longer worth the price of having to rent space from my own mind when I go on vacation."

People in certain careers are more vulnerable to this, military service being one. I worked with a man who had been a Top Gun–type pilot, then a high-ranking officer in the Navy, commanding an elite aerial squadron. He retired without a plan, thinking he would enjoy just puttering around. Four months later, he was in my office with a desperate tone in his voice.

"After twenty-seven years in the Navy, I have no reason to serve and no one to serve," he said. "I've lost my sense of importance, and I've lost my mission." What he really wanted was an assignment, an order. "If I knew the goal, I'd know how to get there," he said, almost pleading. "In the military, I always had specific, clear targets. Give me the target, and I'll get there."

I told him that he did have a mission: designing a new life with meaning and purpose but that it would have to come from within. And that to create it, he would have to dig down into who he really was apart from his Navy years. I could see his face cloud over. "I have no idea where to begin," he said more softly. "I don't even know the questions to ask."

Assessment also helps people who have taken a wrong first (or second) turn in life. Those who know solidly early in life what makes the best use of their talents, what enables them to make a meaningful contribution, are the minority, I would say. Most people take awhile to reach that point. Some drift into a first career.

They can make a go of it, of course, building a career and wealth, but they may not feel satisfied about their work. Many factors explain accidental careers, including the influence of respected professors or mentors, the expectations of or examples set by parents, the press of life's responsibilities, and the need to accept trade-offs. People may feel they lack alternatives or are afraid to follow their instincts.

Some move into work situations by a kind of default. Drifting into a career may have been OK in their twenties. But is it now? Assessment is a time to revisit the reasons we went into these fields or careers and challenge their applicability now. A time to reexamine whether or not we are moving toward fulfillment and if not to retake control. When I give talks or meet with retired men and women who seem unfulfilled or bored, I sometimes walk away wondering, if they had done an assessment before retirement, would it have been different? If they had taken time to know themselves better, would they have taken a different path?

There is a business plan aspect to an assessment, an important one now that we have broken the *one-life, one-career model* and depend less on corporations to think for us. Successful companies clarify goals and reinvent themselves all the time. Why shouldn't individuals? I said at the outset that everyone should think about what they do more like entrepreneurs do. Entrepreneurs continually research and develop ideas for new projects. Assessment is similar to that, but as we say at New Directions, it's "R&D on me." It means taking a new course, Me 101.

When you know your assets and "products" (and the markets for them) as a person, you control your life—now and forever—going forward like entrepreneurs building enterprises. In our post-career years, we must set our own goals, and assessment shows us the way. I should add that in doing this it's important that we don't set ourselves up to fail. Assessment is not about what we wish to be or prefer to think about ourselves. Ideally, it shows us the truth: our liabilities and "debits" on the minus side of our personal ledgers. Assessment can sometimes lead to denial when the truth surfaces, and people may need professional help to work through that.

How do we start? The methods vary. Our clients spend time with our staff psychologist to explore hints and clues that come up

Sculpting a Life

Jean Proulx Dibner is a profile in the power of assessment. Jean, now a highly regarded sculptor in the Boston area, came to New Directions in 1999 after leaving her job managing a large department at Avid Technology. Her career included earlier stints at IBM, Apple Computer, and Digital Equipment Corporation. Jean had reinvented herself before. After working as a reporter right after college, she married and settled into her role as a mother of four children. In her late thirties, as her last child entered school, Jean took an aptitude test and scored off-the-charts high on engineering and spatial intelligence.

Jean consulted with her family and then enrolled in a computer science degree program at a university at night. She earned her degree at age forty and was hired by Digital. Although she hardly knew it, Jean had already gained leadership skills doing community and volunteer work, including raising money for local parks and starting a kindergarten for underprivileged children. She rose quickly from engineering to managing a small group. Over a ten-year period, she was steadily promoted at Digital as a manager and executive. In her last position, as a vice president, she oversaw five hundred employees responsible for 120 products.

While she was at Avid in late 1999, an economic downturn began in the industry. Layoffs were on the table. Jean feared that younger engineers, perhaps with children, would bear the brunt of the reductions in force. "I was ready to do something else anyway," she says, "so I went to the CEO and 'volunteered' to be let go."

Jean already had a passion for sculpture by that point. "One of the things that came out of the aptitude test is that I can easily see and design in three dimensions," she says. She had also taken an adult education course in pottery and found she had a knack for it. She was thrilled to create things from scratch, she says, slowly shaping something with her hands in clay as the idea took form in her mind.

(Continued)

Jean took her love of pottery to work. "I started sitting my engineers down during lunch hour and sculpting their profiles onto mugs," she says. They were a big hit, and she realized what she wanted to do was figurative sculpture. She began more formal training and started sculpting on weekends to satisfy this new passion.

I recall that when Jean came to New Directions, she was keen about moving on fairly quickly. We urged her to slow down and take the assessment process seriously. She did, and as a result, she realized that sculpting, instead of being just a hobby, was something she wanted to do in a serious way. One clue emerged as she reviewed her life story. Jean recalled that in fifth grade she would create little paper sculptures in spare moments as other children completed work or at other points in her daily schedule. She carefully put these folded treasures in her pocket. "I thought they were precious and didn't want to throw them out," she says, "so I carried them around for days. I saw this as another sign of an interest that was there all along."

Jean has since devoted herself full-time to sculpting, showing her work in galleries, museums, and private collections. She is developing a business of selling her pieces. She also started a sculpture center where she teaches others. Jean's work is gaining national recognition, meriting a one-woman show in New York in late 2006.

"Sculpture is a way to comment on what I experience in life," she says. "And creating something others find moving is also a way for me to give back to the world. For all those years I did other things, I didn't really know I had this ability within me. It's wonderful now to be who I truly am and in addition to be appreciated for that. This is the most fulfilling time of my life."

as they talk about their lives. They take written surveys, tell their stories in different forms, network, research, create opportunities, reflect, and dream. But assessment must be flexible. It is about what works, what opens the door, what connects us to our deeper selves. I will go over some practical tools and methods of conducting an assessment in the next chapter. Here, I want to introduce some broader principles behind them.

THE NEUTRAL ZONE

The first principle is the necessity of hitting our inner pause button and being open to possibilities. *Assessment is not necessarily oriented toward specific results.* It is about paying attention. The idea is to generate options without judging them. People start to rediscover themselves when they step on the clutch, disengage, slow down, and decompress from the action. They go into what William Bridges, a respected authority on life change and author, calls *"neutral."*

Assessment takes us down to the core, the nut, of who we are. Bridges urges people to encourage that process by *dis-identifying*; that is, stripping away personal labels, affiliations, titles, and roles.

To do that, we have to go into neutral. In the language of an elementary school crossing guard, assessment is a time to stop, look, and listen. When we do, we come wholly into the present. Two other things may happen. We see life differently and more realistically than when we are rushing. We may also give ourselves permission to feel.

What might it feel like? One man who previously had a pressure-cooker job found the old wheels still turning in his head during assessment. When he managed to disengage them, he told me, "My mind is unclenching the way you'd unclench a tight fist."

Neutral is tough for people used to action and achievement. The temptation can be to take the next train—the next job or activity. In neutral, we let it just rumble through the station. It takes some people a year or two to fully disengage from career goals and find a place where they can bloom as persons. My inclination for years was to hurry people along to the next job after a two- or three-month assessment. Now it seems that more time may often be more practical.

Bridges says that he adapted the term from Arnold van Gennep, an early French anthropologist who, in his study of cultural rites of passage, called the periods in between old and new ways of being a *neutral zone.* A friend of mine who works at a financial services company suggested a more homegrown American metaphor for neutral that I like.

"You have to get to the *sidelines* to see the whole picture," he said. "It's when you're out of the game looking in from a little bit afar that you see other ways to create portfolios." He was able to persuade his company to greatly scale back his schedule so he could become an *executive in residence* at a local business school. It was a great experience for him, he said, adding, "I couldn't have made the case for it successfully if I hadn't gone to the sidelines."

THE STORY OF YOUR LIFE

Another assessment principle is storytelling. Narrative is a powerful tool for self-discovery. People write autobiographies and tell their stories, presenting not just the facts but pausing to reflect on an influential relationship, for example, that was critical to them and why it was. They tell how they felt when a certain important event happened. Some clients keep an informal log or journal to record bits and pieces of their stories. But we don't have to shape the results in a certain direction. What is important is accumulating raw data, the pieces of the puzzle that narrative can reveal.

Storytelling taps into the potential of unconscious mind and creative, nonlinear thinking, which are very useful in assessment. We encourage people to write poetry, draw, paint, or keep a dream journal. We record clients as they give a so-called elevator speech, in which they manage to say who they are and what they are doing in their lives (or want to do) in the space of time it takes to ride an elevator with someone. Then they watch the videotape of their delivery, looking for clues in facial expressions and body language.

Using intuitive methods is not easy for everyone. But I have seen the value people get from paying attention to moods, listening to inner voices, and trusting hunches. I am a very big believer in hunches. Dr. Joyce Brothers said hunches are usually based on facts, filed away just below the conscious level. They are better guides to action than the business world has given them credit for.

ACHIEVEMENTS LEAVE CLUES

Another guiding principle is that accomplishments leave clues. They leave a trail if we are willing to look for it. So we comb our personal histories for what excited and inspired us. We summon a time when we felt good and alive and ask, *what were we doing* in that period of our lives? How did we feel and why? Favorite subjects in school, favorite early jobs, and favorite travels are fair game. So are memories of past inspirations that were put on the back burner as careers were built. The older we get, the further back in our lives we have to look for these clues.

One man who posed a challenge was a client I'll call Frank. A likable but hard-to-peg fellow, he came to New Directions after many not particularly happy years in the import-export business as a chief financial officer. Frank was in his early fifties and looking for another job, not a portfolio lifestyle, but his assessment story resonates.

We set up a focus group of peers to help Frank and one day sat around a table urging him to reach back into his past for ideas. He spoke about a job he held for all of six months twenty years earlier, for the New York State Department of Education. As he did so, Frank's eyes widened, his face lit up, and he leaned forward and spoke with animation. Everyone knew this job had been important to him. Frank said he studied education and once planned to become a teacher. We tried to develop the possibility of a finance position in education, but he dismissed it. "What good would it do?" he asked. "I can't go back to that. That was twenty years ago." Nonsense, we said, and turned it into a search campaign. To make a long story short, Frank ended up in a key financial position at a major university.

You never know where the clues will come from.

What we learn in assessment may reinforce what we already know on many levels. That affirmation can be reassuring. But assessment often reveals new or emerging drives. So it is not just about picking up where you left off in your previous job, vocation, or activity. That is going with your labels; assessment is about peeling them back.

However, people who have been unhappy in their work or life situations can take this point too far. I hear them say that they need to make a complete break with the past. That is a mistake, in my view. Better to think about mining your past for the treasure it holds, building on it, and rolling over the best of your experience, knowledge, and skills into the next phase of your life. Psychologists who have conducted research studies on the issue say that people who display creative continuity with their past lives are the ones who tend to age most successfully.

Finding Our True North

There is a common end point or destination in assessment, and that is getting people in touch with what we call their "PEPC." It's an ugly-duckling acronym, I know, but one we created a long time ago. PEPC stands for *passion, energy, purpose* and *calling*. It becomes our compass as we head into a life portfolio. PEPC is the source of pursuits and missions to replace career goals. Bill Winn, our long-time staff psychologist, calls the whole assessment process a "can opener" to get the lid off people, to uncork the genie of what makes them who they uniquely are.

PEPC is not to be confused with specific skills, talents, or even personality styles. Those are clues to career choices, and they tend to remain relatively constant over time. But personal drives and motivations are different. They do change as we age. Individuals focused on obtaining a certain economic status or title in their thirties may have different drivers in their sixties—such as creating a legacy or taking on an unfulfilled dream.

PEPC is about those sweet spots and hot buttons that tend to stay with us. Dwight Everett left the business world at fifty-five, came to us, and eventually turned to a life portfolio focused around fine woodworking. Everett said that after he invested time, energy, and money in his basement workshop and began turning out pieces of furniture, he discovered a fire in his belly to shape wood. Carpentry was something he had loved doing as a child and young man but had put aside. Everett turned his reclaimed passion into a business, selling high-end, custom-made cabinets and moldings for historic renovations.

"It was there all the time," he said, "but I wasn't paying attention to the pilot light. Now I've turned it up to full flame." Another client offered similar advice. "Find a passion," he said. "You can't retire from a passion."

There is a certain thrill about breaking through to what we really want and having the courage to pursue it. Then, after all the work, it can seem dumbfounding that you did not do it before. That seemed to be how Rick Lukianuk, a former general counsel at two technology companies, felt after leaving the practice of law to become principal of an academy in New Hampshire. Rick loved teaching and taught an introductory law class at the academy. When the former principal resigned, he was offered the job. "I've downsized my career

The Talent Is the Call

I've long been inspired by Ralph Waldo Emerson's faith in people and his belief in the value of knowing our unique call as a basis for choosing our work. The nineteenth-century New England essayist knew this from experience, having chosen the profession of seven of his paternal ancestors, the ministry, only to find it was the *wrong* profession for him. He could not remain a minister in an institution about which he had doubts, so, to the dismay of some friends and supporters, he left the pulpit for a different ministry—that of the pen-and-lecture platform.

There is a passage in Emerson's essay "Spiritual Laws" that embodies in clear language what I am trying to say about assessment. It is about discerning and heeding that inner compass heading or yearning that Emerson believed each person has and refers to as "the call of the power to do something unique."

Each man has his own vocation. The talent is the call. There is one direction in which all space is open to him. He has faculties silently inviting him thither to endless exertion. He is like a ship in a river; he runs against obstructions on every side but one; on that side all obstruction is taken away, and he sweeps serenely over a deepening channel into an infinite sea. By doing his own work, he unfolds himself [Emerson, 1983, p. 310].

Emerson does not say that there is only one kind of work for each of us. Whatever occupation we choose to do, he argued, we must convert into an outlet for our identity. So it's really about having the right attitude, not selecting the type of employment. How do we do this? I find Emerson's answer surprising and just right. He doesn't advise us to consider moralistic principles or duties. Our calling may be that which comes naturally to us, that we "bend" easily to. All we have to do is pay attention, to honor the call. Our talent is the call.

goals, but I've upsided my life," he told me after the move. His enthusiasm must have been apparent to others, including his former colleagues. "People have honestly said, 'Wait a minute, Rick, you
mean . . . you can actually do what you *want* to do?'"

What I call PEPC could be defined as a *calling*, that which we
are summoned to do. There is a hunger for such a purpose, I
believe, in the soul of every human being. Everyone wants to know,
"Why am I here?" "What is to be my contribution?" Finding your
way without a sense of meaning and purpose is like hiking in the
woods with no map, compass, or sense of direction. It can lead to
striving for results that feel empty or worthless once you have them.

How do we know our callings? Others, incidentally, can hold
up a mirror to let us know when our search for vocation has taken
us to firm and solid ground. My friend and Congregational pastor
in Andover, Massachusetts, Rev. Calvin Mutti, told me, "I knew I
was called when I was validated by others. People I respected and
admired told me, 'Cal, you are in the right place.' It helped, lots."

I like the way novelist Frederick Buechner, who is also an
ordained minister, defines *calling*. It is the place, he wrote, "where
our deep gladness meets the needs of the world" (1973, p. 95). We
cannot start with what the world needs, because the world needs
everything. That approach will lead you out and away from yourself, and that over time will weaken your contribution. Instead, start
with the gifts you were given, with what makes you deeply glad.

I try to be a person of faith; I hold the religious idea of a calling dear. Isn't it God's will for us to know why we are here, what
gifts He gave us and how to actualize them? I personally believe
that the strong sense of self-identity that assessment can bring
offers clues to God's ultimate purpose for us. That is not an
abstract belief for me. It's something I think about a lot. "Don't let
me go out of this life without knowing what you want me to do," I
ask in personal prayer. "God, don't let me waste my time. Help me
to know your will and to do it."

A SENSE OF HOPE

People in the process of transition, certainly many people who
try retirement, can feel hopeless. That is yet another reason to
do an assessment. It can be a source of hope. All is not lost. Deep

Questions Asked in Assessment

What is on people's minds as they conduct an assessment? What questions do they ask? What do they worry about? Here are some of the questions that men and women in this process of self-discovery have asked, questions I have heard in one form or another many, many times. I share them so that if you have a similar feeling, hope, or fear, you will know that others have felt the same thing. You may, therefore, feel validated.

- I'm a Type A person. That's what got me to the top. Don't tell me about getting into neutral and taking downtime. I don't want to decompress and I don't need it. My style is to go from high gear to high gear. Does New Directions have a problem with this?
- I've lost my platform and my title. I have no responsibilities, no office, no parking pass, no expense account, no corporate discounts at Hertz or Avis, no secretary, no respect. The phone has stopped ringing. No one wants my advice anymore. How do I cope?
- I don't consider myself creative enough to do an assessment. I never really had any interests outside of work. My job was my life. How do I deal with this? How do I discover new interests or reawaken old interests I never had time for?
- I feel guilty not working, not continuing to earn money to further secure my family. How do I get rid of that? How do I give myself permission to pay attention to me?
- What does a balanced portfolio life really mean? I'm the type that if I get passionate about something, I give it my all. Is this balance? Does it matter?
- I've never felt so without goals in my life. Goals were always set for me by others. Now I need to make my own. How do I do this? Who do I turn to?
- I know I want to help others, to make a difference. But I've never tried to. I'm worried colleagues and friends will think it's strange, think I've gone soft. How do I do this?
- I don't even know the right questions to ask.

motivations can be brought to the surface and real opportunities identified. I received an e-mail from a client who had been in the insurance business for twenty-five years and not long ago took a new job as the year-round director of a camp for disabled children. "The assessment process didn't so much tell me what I wanted to do, because I think I knew it, but it did give me permission to do it," he said. "It gave me the energy and courage to make it happen."

Assessment is not easy. Distinguishing the melody of our lives from the noise of it takes a lot of hard work. And it's a whole lot easier to recognize clues in hindsight, to see what we should have or might have done, than it is to have smarts and bravery to follow clues into the future. But if we hang in there, assessment can put us on the true path. It can open doors to exciting life portfolios never considered or imagined.

CHAPTER NINE

STEPS AND TOOLS IN ASSESSMENT

As we edge from careers to portfolios, assessment helps us imagine what we will do with the gift of extended middle age. It's a chance to eliminate ambivalence, decide what we really want from life, and identify opportunities based on those discoveries, now and for good. But assessment is a strange place, a middle passage between one place and another. Many find it uncomfortable, at least at first. It helps to enter it in the company of others and to have a road map, a set of tools. That is what this chapter is about.

Don't force yourself into the process, because you will not get much out of it if you do. Doing an assessment is not supposed to be a bad-tasting medicine we force down to get better. Get into it wholeheartedly, or consider coming back to it later. Being committed to assessment entails leaving your comfort zone and exploring the unknown. So my first point is simply to embrace change. See it as an opportunity. The shifts in perception and feeling that come with change in our lives, and certainly a big change, can get people thinking more creatively and introspectively. Anthropologists, I have learned, have a saying about it: *meaning comes from contrast.* When you are in the same surroundings all the time, it is often hard to see what is really there. Go to a new place and take in new surroundings, and suddenly you see things that "natives" do not. In assessment, we may stay in much the same surroundings, but we do change our perspective, our angle of vision on our lives, and that makes all the difference. Even changes that are "bad" or negative in character, such as losing a job, offer this potential.

Whole new emotions can be released. I have seen people let go of negative energies they have bottled up for years.

There are multiple levels to an assessment. The first level is sizing up and writing down the core realities we face or needs we have. We call this doing a personal audit. It covers one's health and health care coverage going forward, finances, family relationships, prefered locations, nonnegotiable time commitments, and anything else pertinent to our situation. Next, we look for patterns in our assets—our skills, experience, and knowledge—to see how we might reshape what we have to offer.

The third level is the core of the process. It is the identification of our motivations, the values, beliefs, interests, and goals that drive us. The dreams we hold dear. The missions we see before us. The next level of introspection is that of personal style and preferences, how our personalities might affect options or choices positively or negatively.

Here we acknowledge the limitations that are part of any major work and life decisions. Confirmed introverts, for example, should probably can that plan to turn their second home into a bed and breakfast. In the last major level, we turn outward to explore possible new environments or work and life situations that may hold desired portfolio opportunities.

Here, in collapsed form, are the particulars of the assessment process in six essential approaches or steps, with practical tools for each.

WAYS TO SHIFT INTO NEUTRAL

The first step picks up on a principle discussed in the last chapter. Get into neutral. Sit still. Take a time-out. Give yourself permission to breathe and decompress. I'm no brain scientist, but I think this must turn some kind of switch, because it seems to produce the mental landscape on which portfolio options and clues begin to appear.

According to Bridges, one of the most important rules for assessment is *curb the temptation to act for action's sake*. Such an urge is understandable, but it usually leads to more difficulty. Why? Neutral furthers a critical part of the transition process: bringing the previous chapter of our lives to a conclusion. Closure makes it easier to extract what we have learned from a previous role and apply it to future roles. But we need to *stay* in neutral long enough to reach this point rather than prevent its arrival through premature action. Think of this zone as a middle passage between an ending and a new beginning in your life. That puts neutral in a larger context and gives it a direction. It reassures us that if we stay with it, movement will occur.

The former marketing officer at an insurance company found a novel way to neutral after he left the job. "After I took off, I built a tree house for my ten-year-old daughter," he said. "It was a weekend chore that turned into a two-month project. But I loved it. I could see the results. Three decks, real stairs, electricity, a couch. And while I was building it pretty much with my own hands, very concrete, very satisfying, a corner of my mind was mulling what I had done and what I could still do. It was a strange time, very odd for a seven-to-seven guy like me, but also enormously useful."

The neutral zone is kind of a moratorium on conventional thinking and activity, a time for redefinition. Here are three ways to get into neutral, adapted from one that Bridges recommends in *Transitions*:

- Find a regular time to be alone each day, a time when inner signals can be heard. Pay attention to see if you are suppressing what is bubbling up and figure out a way to cease doing it. And share what you hear and feel and think with others.
- We all learn to suppress our deep desires for some good reasons and many bad ones. Figure out how you habitually do this. Then figure out a way to stop it! In neutral, we don't hold back from thinking about what we really want to do. When you identify something you would really like to move toward, discuss it with others.
- This exercise is morbid but motivating. Think about the dreams, talents, projects, achievements, loves inside of you that would be unexpressed or unrealized if your life ended today. If, at the end of the day you are still alive, and you have done this exercise faithfully, you have the first draft of a portfolio plan.

USE YOUR VERBS

This is a strategy we developed at my company that applies at many turns in the assessment process. Strip away the nouns, the titles, the roles, and the affiliations that we identify ourselves by—and get to your verbs. Nouns close doors. They peg people. Now is not about your last letterhead or what you want to be. It's about what you want *to do!* Strip away old labels and explore your verbs. Verbs are active and dynamic. The clues to the future are in the verbs, not the nouns.

A friend of mine was a sales executive at a company that made electric motors. We talked when that post evaporated. The man said he knew what he wanted *to be:* a senior VP for sales, selling something other than electric motors. We said that such a focus was too limited and urged him to say what he wanted to do. He tried but always came back to his next *status.* We then asked him to name something he did really well, work related or not. He said he was gifted at recalling names. At trade shows, he looked forward to the hospitality receptions because he enjoyed meeting people and could impress them by remembering their names—whether he had met them twenty minutes ago or at last year's reception. He even turned it into a mental trick and could repeat a string of names correctly on demand.

When we said this was a clue, the man asked how he could make money remembering names. We responded that in assessment, it's all about process, and part of that process is sharing what you learn with colleagues, friends, family, and so forth. The client did this. He mentioned his talent to a neighbor, who was a loan officer at a bank who sometimes handled loans in the hospitality business. People in that field, he said, had to be able to remember the names of patrons, and he added that owner-managed businesses such as small hotels, B&Bs, and restaurants could be a great investment. Six months later, our client bought his first restaurant, which he runs along with his wife. I believe he has since bought another one. He loves what he is doing. And he doesn't care that he is not a vice president for sales. How did this all work out? *We got him to use his verbs.*

WRITE A PERSONAL MISSION STATEMENT

In the last chapter, I spoke about PEPC, my acronym for passion, energy, purpose, and calling. This is where our strengths lie, and it holds the strongest possibilities to be developed in the next stage of our lives. Your life portfolio should be centered on what you care the most about, the things that fire you up and allow you to make your best contribution.

So consider writing a PEPC statement as a framework for your life portfolio vision or mission. Our PEPC is reflected in our innate interests, those things we are drawn to instinctively. It can relate to experience or influences that go back to childhood—but it can also take turns in response to powerful life events, solving an inner problem or realizing a need or opportunity. The discipline of putting your ideas down in black and white will help clarify your thinking. It's important to distill the range of personal drivers to a short list of key elements that will make the greatest difference. A simple exercise we have used at New Directions is the starting point:

> Write a statement of mission or higher purpose or vision that encompasses the elements of passion, energy, purpose, and calling that you wish to infuse into your life portfolio. Be prepared to write this statement in several drafts over time.

STANDARD OR WRITTEN ASSESSMENT SURVEYS

There is an abundance of these instruments, including more than twenty-five hundred kinds of personality tests alone. They vary enormously in type and usefulness, just as people vary in how they respond to them. But many people do benefit. And if we look at assessment as the accumulation of data, then tests are merely another source of information. The basic rule is to be honest. First instincts are often most revealing. Remember that taking these tests is a search for truth, not a confirmation of perceptions.

We have devised our own survey that helps predict chances of success in self-employment. We also use Myers-Briggs Type Indicator, Strong Interest Inventory, Edwards Personal Preference Inventory, Hay/McBers Managerial Style Questionnaire, and Change Style Indicator. There are many other excellent instruments, too many to include here. If your needs are limited to exploring the skills needed in a particular job or the nature of a certain field, a government Web site can be useful. It is the U.S. Department of Labor's Occupational Information Network, or O*Net system (www.doleta.gov/programs/onet). It provides an extensive and searchable database of updated information on skill requirements and occupational characteristics.

Our Untapped Riches

John Gardner was an American original: a businessman, foundation executive, public servant, social thinker, professor, and founder of Common Cause. In his book *Self-Renewal* (1963), Gardner said that most people have capacities they never develop. He urges a lifelong exploration of our inner riches—a message that reinforces the portfolio mind-set.

> It is a sad but unarguable fact that most people go through their lives only partially aware of the full range of their abilities. As a boy in California I spent a good deal of time in the Mother Lode country, and like every boy of my age I listened raptly to the tales told by the old-time prospectors in that area, some of them veterans of the Klondike gold rush. Every one of them had at least one good campfire story of a lost gold mine. The details varied: The original discoverer had died in the mine, or had gone crazy, or had been killed in a shooting scrape, or had just walked off thinking the mine worthless. But the central theme was constant: riches left untapped. I have come to believe that those tales offer a paradigm of education as most of us experience it. The mine is worked for a little while and then abandoned. . . .
>
> Exploration of the full range of our own potentialities is not something that we can leave to the chances of life. It is to be pursued systematically to the end of our days. We should look forward to an endless and unpredictable dialogue between our potentialities and the claims of life—not only the claims we encounter, but also the claims we invent. And by the potentialities I mean not just skills, but the full range of capacities for sensing, wondering, learning, understanding, loving, and aspiring.

Fred Phillips came to New Directions after a corporate career heavy on financial responsibilities. Fred was surprised when his assessment scores were low in finance but high in aesthetic and artistic interests, in particular in architecture and historic preservation. That excited him, as he had always had inklings that he

Additional Aids to Assessment

- *Blue-sky brainstorming.* Gather three or four friends for a personal brainstorming session. Choose people you know well, preferably from different parts of your life. These are "blue-sky" sessions: no judgments allowed. There are two goals: churn up opportunities and use feedback to improve your search strategies.
- *Test-drive your fantasy.* Once a direction is identified, a field trip may be appropriate. Visit someone already doing what you are considering. Don't think your way through. Act your way through. Again, experience the space. How does it feel? Devise ways you might try out your dream jobs. This is especially useful when the new path is a dramatic new field.
- *Pull out your report cards.* Read what your teacher wrote about you, not just your grades, from elementary school through high school. There are clues here.
- *Know your stats.* Picture yourself on a card like the athletes have, picture on the front, statistics on the back, no embellishing. The stats tell exactly what positions they should play. What do yours tell you? Use verbs to identify your stats, your competitive edge.

wanted to explore this area but had never done so. The written assessment tests recalled and confirmed that interest. Fred ended up going to graduate school to study historic preservation. There, a professor introduced him to a firm that buys and restores historic buildings—and he signed on.

A PERSONAL BOARD OF ADVISERS

I mentioned the value of having a trusted circle of advisers during the assessment process. We urge portfolio clients to put friends, colleagues, and family members on personal boards of advisers, which serve as assessment sounding boards. They may be in a position to add some depth to your own understanding of certain issues or decisions but at the same time see things from another point of view. Personal boards of advisers are often able to hold up a mirror reflecting a clearer sense of possibilities than you might perceive.

And most of the time, they are stakeholders invested in your success. Again, make sure to choose a broad range of people to be on your board. Include colleagues and friends from your work life as well as those not related to your work. Ask parents, relatives, neighbors, fellow volunteers, or members of boards on which you serve. Cover as much of your life as you can. Ask yourself if college roommates, teachers, coaches, pastors or rabbis, sports buddies, and summer job employers might make a good addition. Adult children are an excellent source of feedback. When considering postcareer options, we need to go beyond work performance measures. As I noted earlier, at New Directions we call it *720-degree feedback,* an expanded version of the traditional *360-degree exercise.* It solicits inputs on values, dreams, and potential legacies.

EXAMINE YOUR LIFE STORY

Give this exercise the time it deserves and stay with it. Stories tell us things that our more rational thinking can miss. If writing is a challenge, consider writing a letter to a friend in which you tell the story of your life. Sift, distill, condense, and organize the "facts" of your life—the hundreds of images, thoughts, recollections, and memories that begin to cross your mind. Highlight central themes, interests, activities, and relationships that matter most to you, the ones that express who you are. Be expansive, boast, but be detailed. Go over highlights, lowlights, and subtleties. Begin with your earliest memories. Describe your parents and grandparents—what they did, who they were, what mattered to them. Later do the same for your spouse and any children. Express your feelings and hopes along the journey. Recall important professors, teachers, mentors, ministers, coaches, or early bosses. The idea is to turn over a memory stone and remember a dream or hope that got put on the back burner as you went about the business of living.

As you do this, remember to *use your verbs.* Describe what you did, not what you were. Relate happiest and saddest events and what was happening at the time. When listing successes or accomplishments, use descriptive or sensory details, about the physical surroundings, for example, to re-create the experience in your mind. If that works, focus on how you felt. Your feelings about that success, your motivation to do it, your engagement during the process, and what it meant to you will reveal key drivers that then can be applied for portfolio purposes.

An autobiography written in the assessment process should cover more than the kinds of landmark events we include on our résumés. Important clues can emerge from "important" hobbies and interests. I met a man who loved boats while he was growing up. He became successful at a technology company, made a fair amount of money, and owned a large sailboat. One of his favorite complaints about his job, he said, was that it interfered with his nautical fun. Eventually, he weaned himself from his first career and bought a small charter business. One summer, I sailed with him. When I asked him how things were going, he was ebullient about his decision to buy the charter business. I asked him why he thought it worked out so well, and without a moment's hesitation, he said, "I grew up and became a kid again."

So look for clues in your hobbies and personal interests. Did you play the piano or another instrument, collect something, enjoy camping, care for a pet or animal? What were your favorite songs and games? Another man I know said that as a boy, seeing the musical *Peter and the Wolf* had an enormous impact on him. "My mother took me when I was six, I think," he says. "But I've never forgotten it." He is now living out his life portfolio, with music as a main theme. He is involved in five or six nonprofit organizations, all music related.

If fitness is important to you, recall what you have done for recreation and exercise. First jobs such as delivering newspapers, selling cookies, or serving as camp counselor rarely show up in our employment histories, but your recollection of how and why you did these activities can be very useful.

Writing your life story can be daunting. It does not have to be long. It only has to be true. One exercise that works for some people is to imagine that you are writing the obituary for the local paper or a school alumni magazine. What would you write about yourself? Not your whole life story, but the most notable things you did with the years that you had at your disposal.

CHAPTER TEN

THE PORTFOLIO FRAME OF MIND

The most powerful resource any of us has in breaking away from careers and executing a major transition is somewhere inside our own noggin. It's our capacity to shift our attitude. William James, a founder of modern psychology, is said to have marveled at the discovery of the simple fact that "a human being can alter his life by altering his attitudes." Changing our mental outlook can have a tremendous positive impact on our lives. It can generate creativity and motivation—two things we need to craft a great life portfolio.

As we move toward a portfolio lifestyle, we need a whole new mind-set. There is no point in retraining your skills if you don't retrain your brain and acquire new habits of thinking—about you and the possibilities in front of you. It helps if we start by acknowledging that how we think influences our behavior unconsciously. Attitudes have more bearing on our life outcomes than we may realize. It has been said that what we expect and believe becomes who we are and what we do. One Harvard study, for example, revealed that people who anticipate memory loss when they age are actually more likely to experience that problem than people who do not.

Similarly, Mayo Clinic researchers who studied a group of thirty-five hundred people found that people who scored high on personality tests for pessimism have a 30 percent higher risk of developing dementia later in life. Those scoring very high on both anxiety and pessimism scales were 40 percent more at risk. Theodore Green, Rhode Island's U.S. senator in the middle years of the last century, got it right when he said that we don't get "old" because we have to give up things we love as we age; rather, we get old *because* we give things up. Green, by the way, retired from the Senate at age ninety-three and was the oldest person to serve in that body until Strom Thurmond broke his record.

The first step is to reject *traditional* expectations about what used to be called retirement. Negative or defeatist attitudes about retirement are downers. But they are so ingrained in our society that, when retirement is mentioned, it's hard not to think of decline, passivity, rest homes, of being pushed out to pasture, or going to seed. And those awful labels we use—*senior citizens, the golden years, the elderly, retirees,* and the like—sap energy and self-esteem *just when we need them to tackle new challenges.* Self-esteem comes from having positive attitudes. This adjustment takes effort, but we have to uproot and toss out "retirement lingo," which implies withdrawal or isolation—and move on.

A friend grumbled recently that Florida is "God's waiting room." I laughed, but the attitude behind the remark—retirement is like a morgue's antechamber—may help explain why people "flunk" retirement. Another subconscious attitude is the sense of entitlement and dependency on being cared for that has crept into our views of retirement over the years. Government benefits and programs have (thank God) dramatically transformed the quality of life for older Americans. But they have also led to a "where's my check?" or "who's going to take care of me?" approach. People with special health or financial realities need and deserve our help. But in general, attitudes of passivity lead nowhere useful.

The good news is that having a self-defeating attitude is not a terminal condition. It can be changed. New attitudes lead to new behaviors. A hopeful, flexible, imaginative mind-set can improve our physical and mental well-being. It can lead us to find joy we may not even know we have. We see over and over that the clients who do best are those who change their attitudes before they change their behaviors. The key is to look forward to this stage of life as a time filled with possibilities, an opportunity to use your wisdom and experience in new ways and for new purposes. Those who take the portfolio route often see it as an adventure, a departing from the past, a voyage with no clear destination. This attitude makes the world pretty exciting.

What, in general, are the elements of this new way of thinking? I think there are at least five major principles or habits of the mind that contribute to it. We must embrace transition with an optimistic attitude, shake up our routine perceptions, cultivate an appreciation of slowness, take leadership of our new enterprise in life, and finally be lifelong learners.

BE OPTIMISTIC AND EMBRACE CHANGE

In reality, the move from job to portfolio is bigger than a job change within a career or even a shift to a new career. It is a *life* change, and those who see it that way do it best. They are ready to pull the curtain on full-time careers and pour their enthusiasm into new adventures and opportunities. So instead of denying change, they believe that it is an opportunity.

A confident, positive attitude is essential in the search for a satisfying life portfolio. A classic story of confidence is that of Fred Smith, who might have been stopped in his tracks if he did not believe in himself. As a Yale undergraduate, he wrote a paper on the concept of an overnight mail delivery service. The professor, Smith once recounted, gave him a C. "It's interesting and well formed," the professor wrote, "but in order to earn better than a C, the idea must be feasible." Smith went on, of course, to found Federal Express. Have you been anywhere for more than a couple of days that you haven't run into a FedEx truck?

Be positive about aging itself. Take pride in your years. If you are carded when you request a "senior discount," don't flinch. Flaunt. Wave that driver's license or Social Security card that proves your eligibility.

With advances in health and longevity, age is truly becoming a state of mind. When people went a more or less straight line from college to the office to the golf course to the coffin, a person's age was key. It told them exactly which stage of life they were in. Americans are living more cyclical lives. A man today who is fifty might be a grandfather or he might be a brand-new father. His wife might be a CEO of a company, or she might have left the business world to teach high school. Attitude is key.

Granted, there is no denying that bodies and minds slow and change as we age. But here is another example of the power of our mind-sets. Why not *reframe* our view of these changes and focus more on the positive aspects of aging? When people turn fifty, they notice they have lost some brain speed and worry if they cannot call names to mind. They may have an actual small decline in gross cognitive power, but they have also *gained* in the bargain. Older adults, researchers say, are better at solving problems, more flexible in their strategies, better able to keep their cool during crises, and better able to bounce back from a bad mood quicker and also have a rich network of associations developed through a lifetime of experiences. And contrary to popular misconceptions, older adults are able to retain new things they learn as well as younger people do.

As Bernard M. Baruch, the early twentieth-century financier and presidential adviser said, "Age is only a number, a cipher for the records. A man can't retire his experience. He must use it. Experience achieves more with less energy and time."

A positive attitude might even help you live longer. In a seven-year study of 1,558 older adults published last year, the University of Texas found people with an upbeat view of life were less likely than pessimists to become frail. So expect to live to be a hundred. Expect to win.

Embracing change positively does not mean it is without challenges. One is the apparent loss of identity that may occur during our transitions. As said previously, many of us live and work in worlds where people identify themselves by titles, industries, companies, and other affiliations. I hear this from new clients all the time:

"I'm an IBM'er."

"I'm a senior partner."

"The size of my office and my salary defined me. What are my new measures?"

"All of my identity was wrapped up in my job."

Portfolio is a time to discover that, in fact, your old job was *not* your identity. It was one of the identities in your overall portfolio of jobs, roles, and relationships that contribute to a sense of who you are. But identity, as such, is deeper than any job. And now is the time to discover that. New labels, new identities, new *anchors* must replace the old.

During this process, I should say that it is OK to be label-less. New attitudes and motivations often require a temporary surrender of the security that self-labels offer.

SHAKE THINGS UP

Develop the ability to reevaluate facts and see things in a new light. We all get into routines that keep us from doing that. But changing even one pattern—taking a new route to work, jogging a different path, or sitting in a new pew in church or temple, for example, can disorient our perceptions and trigger new angles of vision. Doing new and different things seems to get people thinking more creatively. With practice, we can cultivate an attitude of breaking through old thought patterns.

The best way to do that is to change your surroundings and your habits. For example, go to a Wednesday afternoon matinee, change what you wear, the food you eat, the music you listen to, when you go to bed at night or get up in the morning. Attend a religious service in a denomination with which you are unfamiliar. Take in and appreciate the distinctions.

Change your mind-set in other ways. Go back to school, to take a course or get a degree. Take an interim job in a field that interests you or do an internship.

Make sure you get mental exercise, which has been shown to keep people young. Older Americans who take on creative challenges are generally healthier, according to studies done by scientists at George Washington University. They go to the doctors less, are less depressed, and suffer fewer injuries.

Even small changes can make big differences. We once worked with a former controller, a serious, numbers kind of guy—this is a true story—who always wore brown! Brown suits, brown shoes, brown shirts, brown ties. He drove a brown station wagon. He came into the office daily and always seemed to assume the same stance: formal, organized, and detailed. He did not relate much to the other clients. The staff got on his case. The other clients got on his case.

One day, he sauntered into the office in a white turtleneck and gray slacks—no tie, no brown. His entire demeanor was different. The seven of us in the room gaped. Someone managed to make a weak joke, but the client did not care. He looked away, leaned back, and put his arms behind his head and feet on the table. "Forget it," he said. "I don't care anymore. I'm trying something new." Our jaws dropped like falling objects. But our friend was as good as his word. He created another résumé and opened up new options, soon landing a wonderful job, only a mile from home, as executive director of a well-known law firm. He changed his attitude and changed his life.

TAKE IT *SLOW*

Research shows that people think more creatively when they are calm, unhurried, and free from the stress or time pressure that lead to tunnel vision. Tunnel vision blocks alternatives and new possibilities. That may (or may not) help in a crisis, but as an ordinary frame of mind to carry through life it can be a disaster. My best moments of creativity and vision seldom come from high-stress work situations. They occur when I'm in a more relaxed state, often by the water. Perhaps that is why ten million Americans practice some type of meditation. Rooms for people to meditate, sit quietly, stretch,

Lifelong Learners

Developing our curiosity is a part of the portfolio mind-set. If doing that takes you back into a classroom, you will not be alone. America is in the midst of a boom in lifelong learning. About forty million adults now enroll in one or more educational activities every year.

In 1970, students over age thirty-five accounted for 5.5 percent of higher-education enrollment. Today, *one in five* students enrolled at institutions of higher learning is past that age.

The trend holds on the community level as well. The percentage of sixty-six to seventy-four-year-old adults enrolled in at least one adult-ed course more than doubled between 1990 and 2000, to 20 percent. The number of older students will probably continue to grow as adults of all ages upgrade their knowledge or skills through formal university programs, correspondence courses, and employer-provided retraining.

It is also a worldwide phenomenon. Canadians are leading the way, with 6 percent of all adults enrolled in one or more university courses. South Korea ranks second, followed by Australia, and then the United States. But New Zealand, Finland, Norway, Spain, Ireland, and France are not far behind.

or pray are turning up in corporate offices, schools, hospitals, airports, and even prisons the world over.

A lot of people call this mindfulness. Author Carl Honoré has a plainer word: *slowness*. In his book, *In Praise of Slowness* (2004), Honoré describes a global yearning for slowness, prompting, he says, an international *pro-slow* movement. Honoré believes that people are increasingly realizing that the acceleration of life spawned by new technology (and bottom-line pressures driven by global economic competition) has only made us faster—not happier.

Honoré reports that Americans spend 40 percent less time with their children than they did in the 1960s. He also cites British government figures indicating that average working parents spend twice as long dealing with e-mail as playing with their children! The counteraction is building, with pro-slow groups everywhere, Honoré writes. Some, such as the Slow Food Movement, focus on one aspect of life. Others, such as the Sloth Club in Japan, the Society for the Deceleration of Time in the European Union, and the Long Now Foundation in the United States, make a broader case for the slow philosophy.

We have compressed ourselves into multitasking and "zipping" files to speed through life and get more done. The workday doesn't have an end anymore, or at least it doesn't for many people. They make their callbacks on cell phones as they drive or ride home, where, as soon as they get some dinner, they open their laptops and ask themselves, "Now, where was I"?

This is not progress. We will have to change the way we think. If we can shift our minds into lower gear, we will experience better health, enhanced concentration, and what the novelist Milan Kundera, in his novel *Slowness,* calls *the wisdom of slowness.* And there is evidence that some people are decelerating. People are devoting more free time to slow, contemplative hobbies: gardening, reading, model building, beading, pottery, and painting. A perfect example of the slow philosophy is the boom in knitting. The number of book clubs is way up, and parents are rebelling against "accelerated learning" and speed-reading in schools. Homemade crafts are also exploding—a fertile field, by the way, for a small business.

Why do I bring this up? Slowness connects to two essential steps in the portfolio planning process, *neutral* and *weaning.* We incorporate them because they can release the creative juices a productive transition process requires. The alternative—applying a faster-is-better mentality to creating a life portfolio—will lead only to busyness: that chronic complaint of retirees who are mystified that they have no time for this or that. Isn't busyness what you were trying to leave behind? The slow philosophy can be summed up in one word: *balance*. Each one of us should try to make room for slowness. I believe people do better at turning careers into portfolios if they get into a go-slow mode.

YOU'RE THE BOSS NOW

"I've always had someone tell me what to do, when, and sometimes, how to do it. Who do I turn to now? For the first time in my life, I'm boss-less."

Just because you may have worked for someone else for years, don't make the mistake of thinking that you still do. You work for you. Your new title? CEO of your company, of your life. Think and behave like you are the founder of your own enterprise, because that is what you are in portfolio. "You're in the Army now," they told raw recruits during World War II. To those creating or living the portfolio life, I say, "You're a free agent now."

Because there is no longer anyone telling us when or how to move, we must assume that job for ourselves. That means being self-aware, accepting feedback, and learning to pay attention to our moods and inner voices. Driven achievers may have never developed the ability to do that. But it is part of the new attitude we need.

Having a self-employed attitude also means knowing yourself and believing, thinking, and acting independently. A goal to remember is this: determine what it is you deeply want to do and *go* out and create a demand for it. But significantly, this does not mean going it alone. Thinking *for* oneself does not necessarily mean thinking *by* oneself. So collaborate with others, contribute to their needs and efforts, develop ideas, and work on things with friends and colleagues.

With your new corporate title comes new responsibility: you have to *lead* your enterprise. So take charge and take action. Don't just respond to change; initiate it. Studies show that taking control positively influences creativity and productivity. It also increases our self-esteem. Lester Thurow, the renowned economics professor said, during a talk at New Directions, "If you're bold, you may fail. If you're not bold, you *will* fail."

Gerry Beauchamp was bold. A former senior human resources executive at John Hancock, Gerry took an early retirement package at age fifty-three. He was an avid runner, who had completed twenty-seven marathons, so he made this passion—as well as his desire to be more a part of his community—his theme in portfolio. He traded business suits and a sixty-mile-each-way commute for gym shorts and a two-mile run to the YMCA in his community, where he became executive director.

The boldness was taking a job that paid less than half his former salary. With education for his two children in college paid for, Gerry found ways to downsize his financial needs to match. After three years on the new job, he was proud, he told me, to have taken a money-losing operation to break-even status. But the big payoff, he said, "was having this wonderful chance to live and work in my community and spend more time with my kids."

So remember these ten powerful little words: *If it is to be, it is up to me.*

WHEN AMBITION FADES

It is hard to find a better piece of advice for your new attitude than that offered by John Gardner, whose signature theme was self-renewal. I ended the last chapter with a passage he wrote about the "riches left untapped" inside most of us. "Ambition wears out," Gardner once said while addressing a Stanford Business School reunion. "But keep curious. Be interested. Everyone wants to be interesting, but the vitalizing thing is to be interested. Keep a sense of curiosity. Discover new things. Care. Risk failure. Reach out."

I like Gardner's upbeat advice. But the downbeat advice that motivational speaker John Fuhrman offers is just as true. "If you are unwilling to fail," he says, "you've already reached your maximum potential."

Cultivating an attitude of curiosity is part of the entrepreneurial thought process that I have discussed. It's about asking questions, listening to the responses, and never being satisfied with just one answer. If there is something you don't understand about life after you leave your career, ask someone who could point you in the right direction. Always ask and always want to take in new information.

CHAPTER ELEVEN

FIVE PATHS TO A NEW MIND-SET

Some readers may be daunted by the prospect of overhauling their views on life. It's too big, they may feel, too subjective a job. It is, but so is turning an ocean liner a full 360 degrees near its slip, which can be required during a port of call. Several powerful tugboats do it slowly, however, and the job gets done. So here are some "tugboats" to help turn your head around—tools, exercises, and practical approaches that will help you stay positive, generate new ideas, and develop your curiosity and creativity.

GO WITH YOUR STRENGTHS

Don't fight your negative thoughts; *step around them.* Create positive parallel thoughts that can coexist with negatives for a while and eventually replace negatives. For example, don't worry about your personal shortcomings. There are some things that we cannot change. But we can put mental energy into what we do well and what is going well for us. Dwell on your strengths, tend them, magnify them, be led by them, and leverage them. The power of doing that is confirmed by research in the new and growing field called *positive psychology.*

Sometimes we have to *magnify* our strengths to get into a new mind-set. Enrico Caruso did this to conquer stage fright. While he was alone in the wings at the opera one night, a nearby stagehand heard the famous tenor whisper loudly, "Get out of my way! Get out! Get out!" He feared that the singer had gone daft. Caruso later explained to him, "The 'big me' that knows I can sing gets afraid sometimes of the 'little me' that says no, I can't. So I was ordering the little me out of my body!" Don't most of us have a "big person" who longs for greatness and a "little person" who stands in the way? Sometimes a new attitude is all we need to chase the little person off.

THINK FOR YOURSELF

In designing a portfolio life, we must create, invent, develop, and design new paths. To do this, we have to learn to think for ourselves and generate our own possibilities. That means questioning conventional thinking and taking nothing at face value.

Paul Jacobs, the CEO of Qualcom, says he follows that advice because so much of what we read and hear turns out, when examined, to be either false or only partially true. "Whether it is expert advice, what you read in the paper, or what your mother told you, if it is important, take the time to figure out for yourself whether it is really true," he says. The downside, he adds, is that no one will believe you, so you will work harder to sell your idea. "The upside is that everyone else will be running in the wrong direction, so you'll have a more open field in which to innovate. Find the incorrect underlying assumptions and you'll create opportunities."

To challenge conventional responses, you sometimes have to take a topsy-turvy perspective. We had a colleague who was trying to sell a hotel. He was unsuccessful, so he kept lowering the price. We told him to *raise* the price. "You're crazy," he said. "I'll never get an offer that way." He did it, and guess what happened? His strategy pushed his listing into a higher market segment, where it drew a new class of potential buyers. One of them bit, and our colleague sold the hotel at the higher price.

GO WITH YOUR GUT

Bill Warner, founder and former chief executive officer of Avid Technology, mentors technology entrepreneurs and those who bankroll them. "One thing I tell them is they have to go with their gut, with what really matters to them. Success doesn't come from logic. It comes from seeing a connection between what you're doing and something that could have serious meaning and value to others. How do the best entrepreneurs figure that out? The best go with their gut. If the gut feeling is not there, forget about it."

Another visionary, Ken Olsen, founder of Digital Equipment Company, spoke at one of our seminars about entrepreneurship. DEC, as it was known, was king of the mini-computer industry in the 1980s. Someone asked what it takes to successfully start your own business. We all thought the answer would suggest a new and proprietary technology. Wrong. Without hesitation Ken ticked off three requirements. "One, have a passion for your product. Two, know how to manage cash. And three, learn how to delegate."

TRY, FAIL, TRY AGAIN

Success seldom comes without failures. Leave yourself open to make mistakes and learn from them. Entrepreneurs make many mistakes because they see them as obstacles, not barriers. Tom Watson, the founder of IBM, said, "The best way to succeed is to double your failure rate." Be a player. Jump in. Get rejected. Come off the sidelines and learn from the bumps and bruises.

We can learn from the example of people who appeared to be failures but who in fact refused to fail. Here is another marvelous true story, again from the address John Gardner gave at the Stanford Business School:

> The man in question was 53 years old. Most of his adult life had been a losing struggle against debt and misfortune. In military service he received a battlefield injury that denied him the use of his left arm. And he was seized and held in captivity for five years. Later he held two government jobs, succeeding at neither. At 53, he was in prison—and not for the first time. There in prison, he decided to write a book, driven by Heaven knows what motive— boredom, the hope of gain, emotional release, creative impulse, who can say? And the book turned out to be one of the greatest ever written, a book that has enthralled the world for over 350 years. The prisoner was Cervantes; the book *Don Quixote*.

In the world of baseball, one of the biggest failures as catcher was the man who squatted behind the plate for the New York Highlanders in 1906. In one game that year, the opposing team stole

Tickle Your Creativity Bone

Life portfolios don't land in our laps—we create them. So building up our capacity to be creative will serve us well as we design this next chapter of our lives. However, this scares some people, who think they were passed over when all the creativity was handed out. Not so! Each of us has a store of creativity that just needs to be unlocked.

Bill Winn has helped clients do assessments for almost two decades. The typical successful portfolio seeker, he said, is comfortable with unpredictable or random events, willing to try new things, and open to creative ideas or solutions.

Where do you come down on that scale? Consider two useful assessments for measuring your tolerance for change and unconventional thinking: the Change Style Indicator, created by Christopher W. Musselwhite and Robyn D. Ingram (www.discoverylearning.com) and the well-known Myers-Briggs Type Indicator (www.myersbriggs.org).

The challenge, says Dee Hock, founder and former CEO of the VISA credit card company, is not how to get new innovative thoughts *into* our minds but rather how to get out the old ones that are just taking up valuable space. "Every mind is a building filled with archaic furniture," he said. "Clean out a corner of your mind and creativity will instantly fill it." Here are a few techniques that have helped our clients get rid of the cobwebs:

- *Exercise your imagination.* Picture yourself in a new place—financially, emotionally, and perhaps geographically. Go wherever your imagination takes you. Imagine pursuing types of work and play that feel natural and good to you, perhaps ones that you and your partner have chosen. What does it look like, what color is this place, what is the temperature, what does it feel like?
- *Practice using the five senses.* Experts say that using all of our senses helps us think creatively. Test the theory by asking a trusted friend to spend ten minutes leading you blindfolded around a familiar environment. What new things do you notice when forced to rely on new senses?

- *Play the caption game.* Cut out and fold over cartoons from *The New Yorker* so that you and a friend cannot read the captions. Now invent your own.
- *Write three pages a day.* Writing about ourselves is one of the best ways to boost creativity. Start with a master dream list of things you want to achieve in your lifetime. Think big and add to the list whenever you think of something new. Other useful writing exercises include the Hundredth Birthday Review (write a feature story describing your life achievements), the Resolution Log (keep a record of problems you find personally interesting and that would be fulfilling to solve), and Thirty-one Topics (write the numbers one to thirty-one down on a blank page and in each space write one area of your life—personal or professional—you would like to monitor; every day look at the number that corresponds to the date and think of new ways to address the issue).
- *Use new words.* Get used to trying new things by picking an unfamiliar word in the dictionary and using it throughout one day—in speech and writing. Another tool for this is to do a crossword puzzle every day. The clues in crossword puzzles often force you to think differently or come at a problem from a different angle. (When I did a recent puzzle, I had to find words suggested by these clues: "greens course," "car bomb," and "up." The solutions, "salad," "Edsel," and "at-bat" tested my creative thinking. My batting average on that particular set of guesses was only .333, I might add.)
- *Count the "F's."* Count the F's in the following sentence. Count them *only once;* do not go back and count them again.

**FINISHED FILES ARE THE RE-
SULT OF YEARS OF SCIENTIF-
IC STUDY COMBINED WITH THE
EXPERIENCE OF MANY YEARS.**

How many did you find? There are six F's in the sentence, but the average person only spots three of them. Most people

(Continued)

don't count the F's in the three "of's." Some say it's because
we skim over small unnecessary words; others claim the human
brain tends to see the F in "of" as a V, because it's pronounced
that way. Either way, this exercise offers a perfect example of
the necessity of slowing down and looking at things in new and
creative ways.

For more ideas, contact the Creative Thinking Association
of America (www.thinkoutofthebox.com).

thirteen bases while he was catching—a record of ineptitude that has
never been broken. Can you imagine how this man felt when he
was dismissed from the team a short while later? But he didn't give
up on the game he loved. He became a coach, then a manager,
then a general manager, and he ended up helping to reshape the
national pasttime.

His name was Branch Rickey. As general manager of the
St. Louis Cardinals, Rickey presided over the "Gashouse Gang" of
the 1930s and 1940s, which was the second most powerful dynasty
after the New York Yankees. He invented the use of farm teams to
recruit minor-league players, introduced innovations to spring training, and in 1947 achieved the triumph for which he is remembered.
As team manager for the Brooklyn Dodgers, Rickey went against
the wishes of baseball's commissioner and personally signed Jackie
Robinson, the first African American to play in the major leagues,
to be his third baseman. Rickey's bravery desegrated the game of
baseball for good. (He just never played catcher again.)

CONNECT WITH OTHERS

It's vital to connect with others—friends, family members, neighbors, and colleagues—during times of major change. Having the
support of others helps stabilize the process of finding and getting
back to our core values and is often the impetus we need to move
forward. If your attitude about your postcareer life is defensive or
a source of guilt or shame, you probably will not make a lunch date
to talk about it with a friend. But if you follow some of the paths

suggested in this book and begin to see that you are moving to become the person you want to be, you will. The connections that result from reaching out move the process along more quickly.

Developing a psychological or emotional connection with people who have gone before us can also have great value during a transition, especially when the lives we explore are those of our personal links to the past—our forebears. Others must agree. People are unearthing their family roots in record numbers. There are more than twelve thousand books and five thousand magazines devoted to genealogy, not to mention one million pages of genealogical data one can search via the Internet.

This boom personally fascinates me. I am sure the fact that such vast amounts of genealogical data are now more accessible is one reason, but something more powerful is evident. Perhaps we are coming to realize that family history deepens personal growth and aids the process of identifying core values. Knowing your family tree, it's been said, helps make you whole. Ancestors have also been called *magic mirrors* that reflect past, present, and future. In discovering them, we may discover ourselves.

I felt that urge to connect with the past recently. My wife, Linda, and I went to a family funeral in a town about forty-five minutes by car from Boston. As I drove home afterward, I was in a reflective mood and my cell phone and radio were uncharacteristically off. I happened to notice a historic marker in the old mill town of Billerica that announced the presence of the Danforth Homestead. That struck me. Danforth is my middle name.

A bit of research disclosed that I was related to more Danforths who had lived in that area than I could have imagined. Some seventeen were buried there in the South Burying Ground, which goes back to 1663. The next Saturday, we returned to Billerica with a sketch of the old cemetery, which we had obtained via the Internet.

As we walked around, struggling to read the faded names on the ravaged tombstones, we discovered one Danforth, then another, and another, sometimes pushing back tree branches to read the dates, the full names, the places of birth and death. I am from these people, I thought. I wanted to plant flowers, to bring flags, to help keep the place up. There was no great insight perhaps, no discovery, but I came away with something better: a sense of gratitude, humility, and connection. We will go back.

CHAPTER TWELVE

ANCHORS IN A SEA OF CHANGE

Let's retrace the process I have sketched so far. You recognized a desire to open a new chapter in your life, summoned the will to act, and began to wean yourself from your primary career. You did an assessment, during which you went into neutral and tuned up your intuitive mind. By different ways and methods, you came to grips with your passions and purposes, and then, based on these, you identified broad goals and opportunities. You adopted a positive, possibility-generating mind-set about the future, checking the habit of thinking that how it has been, or is now, is how it must be.

In many respects, the most challenging part of the process is over—but not the process itself. Now you need to turn broad goals and desired environments or situations into defined, targeted, short- and long-term goals and create a set of action steps to achieve them.

What you need is a written plan with a logical sequence of steps, fallback options, and a few blue-sky build-outs just for fun. Put it down on paper. It's the business plan of your new company: Me, Inc.

Good planning is central to any major life transition. You may feel tempted to wing it, especially if your assessment boosted your confidence and you know where you want to go. Resist that temptation! There is a spontaneous aspect to winging it, and I am all for spontaneity. But at its best, "planning on the fly," as we call it, means *adapting an existing plan,* not working without a plan. If you don't create a *new* plan, you may slip back, without realizing it, to a preconceived one in your mind.

Older plans and strategies don't guide us well as we mature. Carl Jung, a founder of analytic psychology, knew that. Most people, he wrote, step into later midlife with "the false assumption that our [past] truths and ideals will serve us as hitherto. But we cannot live the afternoon of life according to the program of life's morning; for what was great in the morning will be little at evening, and what in the morning was true will at evening have become a lie" (1969, p. 784).

Know Where You're Going

People without a plan are like Alice as she wandered through Wonderland. Do you remember? Alice came to a fork in the path, with trails heading off in two directions. She saw a Cheshire cat in a tree and asked which road to take. The cat asked Alice *where* she wanted to go. Alice said she did not know.

"Then," said the cat, "it doesn't matter" (Carroll, 2002, p. 53).

If Lewis Carroll isn't your cup of tea, then perhaps baseball's Yogi Berra will persuade you. "If you don't know where you're going," the catcher said, "you might not get there."

Well, nobody wants to end up "not there." The many behavioral studies I see in the course of my work with people in transition bear out what I am saying. Studies of pre-retirement planning show that people who engage in a higher number of planning activities prior to retirement are later *significantly more involved* in situations that promote social interaction and stimulate thinking. They also read more, they travel more, and they are more engaged in social and religious activities. Research shows that planning is a good indicator of satisfaction in retirement.

Unfortunately, many people discover that they did not plan adequately for a second wind during their postcareer years. The winds of change are blowing all right. But their sails are not up. This is understandable to some extent. People who leave longtime life structures for traditional retirement or another path may feel that they now lack goals. They had clear goals in school. They did well and graduated. They had clear goals in their careers. They were promoted, made more money, and accepted increased responsibility. Now with the familiar supports and expectations of a career stripped away, there are no clear goals and no one to set

"If we take a late retirement and an early death, we'll just squeak by."

them for you. Many goal-less people put considerable energy into aligning and planning their financial resources and assets. But they forget about the most precious asset any of us owns: our time.

It's surprising but true that some successful senior executives and managers don't do well at planning their own lives. In business, one must deal continually with strategic planning, plans for product rollouts, long- and short-term budgets, and plans for deploying people and resources. But—speaking as a founder of a company— I have learned that when it comes to planning for ourselves, too many of us are less proactive, less forward thinking. A financial services executive told me, "Successful retirement involves thought processes and planning for which most of us receive little or no preparation or training."

There may be a fear or a psychological factor that stalls planning as well. According to a story in the *Wall Street Journal,* one-fourth of CEOs make no retirement preparations because they cannot face the "haunting specter of no longer being the highest boss." People who have had successful careers may also fear trying something new; they may fear criticism, failure, or simply leaving their comfort zone. But when fear of failure blocks us from planning, it becomes a self-fulfilling prophecy.

"Here's what happened to me when I left my company with no plan and no goals," said a former client, once a senior manager at a large computer manufacturer. "Retirement looks great. . . . So far so good. . . . Now, wait a minute, I'm getting a little antsy. . . . Oops, what have I done?" His problem, as he readily admits, was not reexamining an assumption made by some people who know they have solid financial benefits for retirement. He expected retirement to evolve on its own.

Change is inevitable. So plan for it and learn to see it as something positive. I firmly believe that there is no need for anyone to be caught flat-footed by change in careers and life plans, not knowing where to go next. If preparations are made in advance, when change comes, another job will be closer at hand, or the networks for portfolio will be further advanced. By strategically placing islands in the sea of change, you will always be equipped to move forward, even in the face of sudden or significant change. No one likes to be in a situation where next steps are illusive, and entering traditional retirement can feel like that. "I'm back to square one," we have heard. "How did this happen?" It happened because the individual did not think about it. Goals and plans can help make that feeling of returning to square one a permanent, distant memory.

GOALS PREPARE US FOR CHANGE

Goals are our main guides in planning. Now is our chance to break free from the past and name our new destinations. But this must be done before we decide how to get there. In the case of planning a life portfolio, the assessment you undertook helped you identify big-picture life goals. The planning process forces you to really explore, refine, and revise those goals, to see them in a realistic light and perhaps test them out, then distill from them the basics for a plan of action.

Goal setting is as valuable to individuals as it is to businesses. We replace losses with new vision and new purposes. Goals give us a reason and—more important—the confidence to drop what does not fit anymore and put our energies into something new and more fulfilling. Goals, both large and small, *prepare* you for change. They are motivators in transition. They also help us keep on a long-term track, focused on what is important. This can be especially important in times of trouble.

When setting goals, one might start with, "What feels right?" or "What's missing in my life?" or "Do I have unfinished business?" Choose goals that are consistent with the way you see yourself. Break larger life goals down into achievable objectives. The old proverb remains true: yard by yard, life is hard; but inch by inch, it's a cinch.

What are life goals? They are deeply felt aspirations and hopes that define our values and how we want to live our lives. They are those places where we choose to put our energies. Life goals, after being tested and redefined during assessment, become the framework of your portfolio. In the portfolio approach, it is also important to have multiple goals in each of the slices of the portfolio pie to prepare for the inevitable and unexpected bumps and twists in the road. Maintaining a variety of goals helps prepare you for setbacks. If you are working toward several complementary goals and happen to stall on one of them, you are not out of the game. You will be prepared to take a different path.

Goals are also important because they lead to the pleasure of accomplishment. How fantastic it is to be able to reach a goal—or exceed it. It builds morale, self-esteem, and confidence, often so fragile during personal transitions. Building in opportunities to say, "I made a tiny step toward my goal today" must be part of any plan.

Goal setting can be challenging to those who are not accustomed to being self-starters or who did not have to set their own daily, weekly, or yearly objectives. But set goals you must, because people who lack goals have difficulty creating a meaningful life when familiar props are pulled away. "The first year after I left my company was a throwaway," a client told us. "The second year was also a letdown, because I hadn't planned ahead." He had been so engrossed in his job, he said, that he hadn't taken the time to look beyond it. Goals help organize the present, the infrastructure of our lives. When you leave behind something that has been your long-term anchor and primary affiliation, as this client had, you may sense that your platform has gone away. Setting short-term goals helps to organize the present as you work to identify new identities.

Goals Yield Purpose

Goals and plans give purpose. Even if your higher ideals are not reached, the desire to realize them brings meaning to each day. Goals are not only targets and objectives. They are also compasses and navigational aids that tell us the general direction we want to go. Moving in that direction is progress!

Don't do all this alone. Setting goals *for* yourself does not demand that you do it *by* yourself. Your new team may no longer be composed mainly of work colleagues but may include people involved in all aspects of your life, old and new friends, family members, mentors, and advisers. One immediate goal should be to identify who is on your new team.

Rich Gula, a former client, gives this advice: "Make a list of the people you admire, and why. You have to have some models to inspire you to keep your dream alive. Nobody will do it for you. No one else really can care as much as you do about the endeavor of creating a unique future path for your personal and professional life. But there are friends out there who respect what you are trying to do, and they do care. You have to keep in touch with them, continually."

Gula reinforces what I tell clients all the time. We have to manage our own lives because no one else is going to do it for us. But we don't have to do it (nor can we) alone. Others stand ready to help.

There is, it's true, a kind of paradox about goals. We do need them to anchor and guide us. But we cannot be slaves to them. Our priorities, preferences, and values, the things that motivate and drive us, change as we grow. So we have to be willing to accept that certain goals no longer serve us. We need to adapt, revise, or even junk them in favor of new goals that suit the next step in our journey.

It's easy to get stuck on the idea that there are fixed measures of success we should bend toward with all our might. Maybe it's something men do more than women, but some people keep a scorecard of their progress and check it constantly. We do for so long that we think our world will change when we get there, that bells and whistles will go off. How many individuals have sat across from me and told me that they attained these goals—and lost other real opportunities to be happy, like knowing their own children? They accomplished their goals, darn it, but that didn't satisfy. Remember that goals must be constantly challenged, revised, and adapted to new situations. Emerson knew this and said it beautifully. "Not in his goals," he wrote, "but in his transitions is man great" (1965, p. 38).

THE FOUNDATION OF A PORTFOLIO PLAN

As I mentioned, to accomplish new goals developed through the assessment process, you need a written plan. If ideas do not get from the head to paper, they will not be developed or tested and you will not be committed to them. Use the model of a business plan to draft a portfolio plan. It's a structure and a sequence of steps that complement and reinforce one another. A good plan is realistic, keyed to opportunities in the real world, and specific.

In the remainder of this chapter, I am going to go over the first step—choosing how you will allocate your time. Like all first steps, it determines the direction and tone of all that follows. Think of it as *strategic planning* and the later steps that help you plan how to achieve your goals as *tactical planning*.

Allocation builds on what you have learned in assessment. Having done an assessment, you have a clear picture of your core motivators, or PEPC, which, again, stands for passion, energy, purpose, and calling. In this first step, we try to locate your motivators across the five portfolio components or allocations.

- Vocational and professional pursuits; income production
- Ongoing learning; self-development; spiritual growth
- Avocation; recreation; play
- Relationships with family and friends
- Giving back; community and humanitarian work

You may wish to use the five-slice pie model we use in the Life Portfolio Program. Take a plain sheet of paper and trace a large circle on it (something similar in size to a coffee can). The space inside the circle represents your time. Not all your time—you can ignore the time you spend eating, sleeping, shopping for groceries, or any other daily maintenance activities. The time we want to focus on is the time you spend in purposeful activities as you pursue the portfolio lifestyle.

Now look at the list of allocation categories. Think about each one and how you want or need to address it in this new phase of your life. Do you plan to work part-time? Then draw a line dividing your "pie" appropriately and write Vocational in one section. Do you plan to spend time in the great outdoors? Then carve out a hefty section for Recreation. Are you planning on returning to the piano? Becoming more involved in your community or church? Spending more time with your family? You get the picture. Divide your pie chart into sections that show how you would like to spend your time going forward, not forever, but at least for the near term. Fill out this chart as best you can. Now step back and take a look. No doubt your first pass at allocation will appear somewhat lopsided. That's OK. The point is to help you flesh out this chart so that it reflects the real you and reveals action steps that will help you achieve your goals.

Use a pencil! As you think about your values and drivers, you will want to tinker with your allocations, adding more time here, subtracting time there. In choosing your allocations, remember to maintain balance among them. I believe all five elements are necessary in some proportions for a balanced and happy portfolio lifestyle (see Figure 12.1 for an example).

Once you get your allocations distributed to your satisfaction, add specific or interim goals in each of the areas. These should be as realistic and detailed as possible, keyed to real opportunities, and if possible supported by action items. This is where you add in more concrete plans or dreams. In the Vocational section, indicate whether you are planning on pursuing board seats, a part-time job, or simply maintaining membership in professional organizations. In Recreation, write your plans to perfect your downhill skiing or hike the Appalachian Trail. If you want to go back to school, jot that down in Ongoing Learning, and so forth. Put at least one activity in each section of the pie. Listing your desired activities will in itself help expose your values and drivers, but consider how allocations to one area will affect your desire to achieve

FIGURE 12.1. ALLOCATION CATEGORIES: STRATEGIC PLANNING.

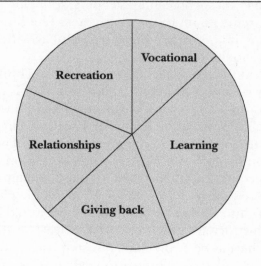

balance in the whole. If you have nine activities planned for recreation and none planned for learning, then in the long run your portfolio will lack the balance needed for continual growth. And again, use a pencil so you can make changes (see Figure 12.2 for an example).

You don't need to think of this division of your time as permanent. Things will change in your life, and interests and your portfolio will adapt as you embrace these changes. Like any good strategic plan, a portfolio is flexible and malleable, but it should always point toward the ultimate aim, in this case an allocation of your time that expresses your values and desires.

THE SPIRIT, NOT THE LETTER, OF YOUR PLAN

Although it is important to have a structured plan, we can also have a less-structured portfolio schedule. The process is going to unfold in fits and starts in any case. The key thing is to see the difference between flexibility and randomness. Opportunities may indeed seem to present themselves in serendipitous ways, but we

FIGURE 12.2. ALLOCATION CATEGORIES: TACTICAL PLANNING.

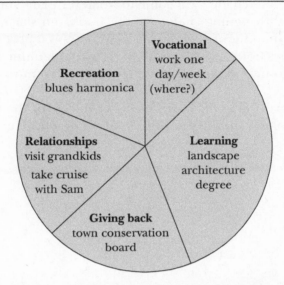

can also create our serendipity by putting ourselves in the right place, with the right attitude, at the right time. Planting seeds for future gardens also helps. Good luck is just the intersection of opportunity and preparation. You may not be able to predetermine the opportunities, but you can prepare for the likelihood that an opportunity will present itself.

I have not mentioned goofing off yet, but that too is part of portfolio. We all need rest, and people who are transitioning out of long careers may need more downtime than others to recover their bearings. No plans or goals for a while. That of course is fine. In fact, anticipating this need and planning for it by building weaning into the plan can actually enrich the process of slowing down. By planning ahead, you will be prepared to come out of neutral with a more meaningful, relaxed, but balanced lifestyle.

Even with a plan, shifting from the highly structured workaday world to a self-structured portfolio schedule will have rough spots. So if you can, start now, today, to think about and write down your hopes and goals, your general plans and expectations. The important thing is not to create a detailed long-range plan at this point but rather to keep that agenda, that outlook, on the back burner of your mind. One thing is certain. Change will come to your life, and change will come to whatever plans you have. But as I said in the opening chapter of this book, our starting premise is that the shaping of your prime-time years is a process, not an event. It does not happen overnight. It takes planning ahead and openness to new ideas and patience—patience most of all with oneself.

In the next chapter, I will discuss the rest of the process in which you plan your life portfolio in more practical terms.

CHAPTER THIRTEEN

PLANNING FOR SUCCESS

I explained in the previous chapter how important it is to create a written life portfolio plan based on the model of a business plan. We also considered the first strategic step in formulating a plan, which is allocating our time to the pillars of a life portfolio. Now let's continue drawing up a life portfolio plan.

Taking the knowledge that we gained in assessment about our dreams and translating this into an action plan is challenging, but there are tactics that can help you succeed. Creating a plan will inform and advance your thinking about your life portfolio, and it will also lead to a detailed list of action items and achievable goals.

This chapter will look at four remaining steps in the planning process:

- Identify working goals based on portfolio allocations.
- Explore and generate opportunities.
- Analyze and counter gaps.
- Build in ways to revisit, reflect, and rebalance.

We focused on configuring our five portfolio allocations in Chapter Twelve. Now you need to bring more order to the mixture of short- and long-term working goals that you identified in each category. After completing a first pass through this sorting process, you will also have clear action steps to move you forward. So now it's time to get organized and get moving!

DEVELOP YOUR WORKING GOALS

The pie chart you filled out (see Figures 12.1 and 12.2 in the previous chapter) gives you a good start on developing your goals for your portfolio lifestyle. Now it's time to elaborate and expand your goals in the five areas as much as you can. This is a time for dreaming and thinking. Prioritizing and applying a reality check come later. Allow yourself enough time to develop a mental state that is open to new possibilities. Take the time to let your subconscious help figure out what it is you want to do. This can be a scary thing to do. Don't let the concept of "retirement" creep into your thinking, and don't succumb to the fear of trying something new. Enroll the whole family in the process. Particularly ask your children; they know you better than you think.

Focus on how you are going to spend your time. You may have many years ahead, possibly as many as forty. Ask yourself the following questions:

- What opportunities am I going to develop to satisfy and develop my skills and ambitions?
- What commitments do I want to make to my friends and community?
- What opportunities and adventures did I set aside when I started my career?
- What are my kids (or my spouse) doing that I wish I could do?

Reflect on your own experience and list what you are currently doing. Then cross out those items that in an ideal world you would no longer be doing and keep only those that you want to continue or those you want to expand. Consider situations, environments, and scenarios, not well-defined daily activities. For now, try not to be constrained by external realities. We will factor those in later. Listen to your internal drivers. You are trying to identify your motivators. What excites and motivates you? When do you feel most alive?

Get to know yourself well enough to understand what the motivators are. Think about what makes a difference for you. Is it important that you be part of an organization or do you prefer to work independently? Is working with a certain kind of person or people a factor? Is there a certain kind of organization that you would like to get involved with? Again, focus more on environments and conditions than on the specifics with regard to this role or that role, this location or that location.

- *Dream.* Write down past and present dreams, met, partially met, or not met. Some may be as basic as learning how to use a spreadsheet on a PC or playing the piano. No aspirations are too large or too small. Be optimistic. Picture the world as a good place, perhaps one you can make better.
- *Play.* Let your mind roam. Whatever limitations you have are likely ones you created and exist only in your mind. Throw them off. What have you always wanted to do? What did you most love to do when you were a child? Whom did you most admire? Something happens when you get a clear internal picture of what you want. It programs your mind and body to achieve that goal.
- *Visualize your ideal lifestyle.* Imagine your ideal lifestyle five, fifteen, twenty-five years up the road. Ask the family. Picture where you might be at the beginning of the day—the place, the furnishings, the world just outside. Touch something. Are you involved in work, a hobby, or other interest? What is it? Are you at home or work, or does it matter? What is the place or building like? What is your space like? Who is there? What kind of people? What will you do? With whom? You pick up something on the way home. What is it? Who is at home when you get there? What do you do in the evening? Why do you feel good about today? How do you get ready for tomorrow?
- *Create your ideal day.* Beginning to end, where would you go? Where would you be? With whom? Accentuate the sense of the day. Let your mind go. Design an environment that will bring out the best of all that you are as a person. Where would you be—in the woods, on the ocean, in a library, moving in a dance studio? Creating in a painter's hideaway or a personal woodworking shop? What tools would you have—an art pad, paints, music, a computer, a telephone? What support people would you want around you to make sure you achieve and create all that you desire in your life?
- *Ask yourself* why? If, for example, you just say you want to be wealthy, that is a goal, but it does not tell your brain much. If you

understand *why* you want to be wealthy, what it would mean to you, you will be much more motivated to get there. Why to do something can be much more important than how to do it. If you get a big enough why, you can always figure out the how. If you have enough reasons, you can do virtually anything.

• *Resurface your goals.* Consider old goals, ones that you had to put on a back burner or let go altogether earlier in your life and rebuild the connection.

Try the following exercise to get your creative juices flowing:

• Imagine your life five years from now. Anticipate and consider the changes that are likely to affect your profession, your place in it, how those changes might affect your personal satisfaction, and the consequences for this and other parts of your life.
• Imagine what your experience might be like if you made no change in direction. Consider both the positive and negative consequences of remaining closely tied to your current profession.
• Imagine the kinds of things you might like to be doing at a point in the future if you were not constrained by circumstance. This is most helpful if you can get down to the level of daily activities and envision what life might be like under ideal conditions. Try to come up with a new way of thinking about who you are and what you have to offer.

If you are still having trouble filling out the portfolio pie, experiment with this exercise:

• Are there possessions you want to acquire or retain in this stage of your life?
• What interests and activities will create meaning and enjoyment in your life?
• How do you want to feel about yourself, your life, and your relationships?

Use your answers as a reality check for the authenticity of the options you have selected and how well they fit with other aspirations. Try options on for size. Take field trips. Arrange to visit or job-shadow individuals doing things about which you have an interest. Record your results.

Brainstorm as many potential options as you can imagine related to the five life portfolio categories (Vocational, Ongoing learning, Giving back, Relationships, Recreation). Write the options down on paper as succinctly as possible. As I mentioned, you can rank and prioritize them later in the process. Continue brainstorming until your portfolio pie is overflowing with ideas. Now, equipped with this preliminary pie, you can start to explore possibilities and identify opportunities, eventually transforming some of these goals and aspirations into reality.

Explore Your Possibilities

The next step is to explore a range of possibilities and opportunities to support the stated goals. The purpose here is to conceive options, try them on for size, and narrow the list to a few around which goals can be prioritized and pursued.

Here are some actions I have found to be helpful in exploring possibilities. I call them Inside, Outside, and Leapfrog. The proximity of options to your current activities determines the best approach for you.

- *Inside.* If you are considering something closely related to your profession or existing interests, an inside strategy is in order. In this strategy, learning about the possibilities, if that is needed at all, will require contacts close to the portion of your network related to your professional activity. This would be true of a change of position or organization, but within the same sector.
- *Outside.* If you are contemplating a change of industry or discipline, an outside strategy might suit you better. An outside strategy requires reaching further into your network. A chain of contacts may be needed to get to the kind of information that would be most helpful in exploring these possibilities.
- *Leapfrog.* If you are thinking about trying something completely new, moving to altogether new terrain, employ a leapfrog strategy. Most likely, this will require moving beyond your personal network, and the quicker you can accomplish this, the

more likely you will find the necessary sources to explore potential options.

But if you don't yet know what opportunities you would like to pursue, you might want to take an interim step, gather a little more input, and try something that will help you identify a range of possibilities to explore to determine if they are indeed valid opportunities. Opportunities need to be *created*, not just found.

The following are some techniques you can use to jump-start your creativity.

- *Brainstorm.* Good ideas come out of a lot of ideas. Get the right participants in the room. Create a clear statement of the problem and don't critique or debate ideas. Build on stated ideas and jump to others. Keep a record for later evaluation.
- *Find models.* Listen to people who have been there. Get the context as well as the details. Understand their point of view. What are the issues, requirements, challenges, and opportunities? Is closer inspection warranted? You may be further inspired or turned off by being closer to the action. Either way, you will have learned more about the opportunity and more about yourself.
- *Shadow.* Experience "a day in the life of." Select subjects and time frames carefully to learn about typical situations. Know when to ask questions and when to avoid interference. Consider how your presence may have altered the experience. Debrief after the fact, not during.
- *Tryouts.* Arrange to volunteer or to act in an interim capacity for a designated amount of time. You can check out the business or organization—while they check you out. Volunteering sometimes puts you on the inside track for a permanent role.
- *Expand an interest.* Take something that you are already involved in and use it as a lever or expand a current involvement, such as being on a nonprofit board or some other activity. This is an excellent way to move in a new direction. The principle is that there is already something that you know about and are doing that you might consider pursuing on a more structured basis or from another angle.

A key component in identifying real opportunities is sharing your thoughts and dreams with others. Start with your board of advisers and get their feedback. Develop a brief description of your goals and aspirations and share it with others as often as you can.

IDENTIFY GAPS AND MAKE ADJUSTMENTS

The next step is to identify the gaps. Start by comparing your list of goals with your list of opportunities. For those goals that have no matching opportunity, you will have to do some more research to uncover potential opportunities. There may be opportunities out there that you just have not uncovered yet, or you may be lacking the education or experience that would be needed to move ahead in a certain area.

Will your relationships suffer or be enriched? Can you handle the loss of identity from changes in titles, affiliations, and labels? What about where you live and enact your plan? Is it appropriate? What if you no longer have an office? Do you have enough space? Do you see a problem in time management? Are there gaps in your skill level to do your plan or the resources that will be available to you? Are you dealing with all the trade-offs? Some goals may turn out to be working at cross-purposes and may require trade-offs.

For each of your goals, ask the following questions. The purpose of this exercise is to bring into focus the alignment between the possibilities you have identified and your personal drivers, external realities, and other factors important to success. Any gaps need to be assessed to determine if they are critical, and if they are, how they will be closed.

- How closely does this option line up with my decision drivers? If some requirements are not met, how important are they to the satisfaction and meaning I will take from the activity? What negative consequences could result from this compromise?
- How well does this option fit my skills, knowledge, experience, credentials, values, and preferences? How will I gain or compensate for what is missing?
- Does this option conflict with any of the external realities I have identified? How will I reconcile the two?

- What information (or other resources) do I need that I don't have in order to better understand this option and how best to pursue it? Where can I get them?
- What network connections will I need to make to move in this direction? Do I know these people myself or who can lead me to them?
- What is a realistic assessment of the odds that I can pull this off and how long might it take? Am I willing to patiently stick with the process in order to achieve this goal?

Record your answers to these questions. If the hurdles seem higher than you imagined, now is the time to consider carefully how important this goal is to the success of your life portfolio. If you are passionate about any given option, regardless of the degree of difficulty in attaining it, you will not give up on it easily— go for it!

In some cases, internal drivers will need to be reconciled with external realities. This may require compromises of various types. An examination of external realities may lead to a modification of an activity to fit a particular constraint or to an adjustment of a constraint in order to limit its impact on the targeted activity. Either way, the two forces, external factors and personal drivers, interact to give shape to life portfolio allocations.

Trade-off decisions may be needed when market conditions or other factors do not make available the precise option you have targeted. Similarly, to achieve one objective, you may need to give ground on another. In order to accomplish a key element of your life portfolio, it may be necessary to engage in a complementary activity that would not otherwise be a part of your portfolio. We refer to such activities as *enablers* because they make desirable activities possible, even though they are not in their own right targeted objectives.

Concessions may also be required to reconcile internal drivers with external realities. These may range from short-term allowances to longer-term give-ups, made necessary by either transitory or enduring constraints. In some instances, you may find that a learning curve is needed to rise to the level of performance or contribution you desire. In this case, a decision to work your way up may reflect a compromise willingly made to reach the desired outcome.

In order to match goals with opportunities, list the obstacles or impediments that prevent you from pursuing that goal. Only by identifying what is stopping you can you move forward. What price will you be willing to pay to secure your ideal portfolio? You may need to downsize real estate, autos, clubs, discretionary living privileges, and the like. How much free time are you willing to sacrifice to keep working to provide ongoing income? Hard questions. Even with formal directorships and nonvolunteering, flexibility will have to be practiced. You can't have it both ways.

Respond to these gaps or trade-offs by developing ways to coexist or cope with them or line up resources to fill them. In addition, revise and adjust your goals, your plan, or both. If necessary, redraw your portfolio pie. Redraw it to reflect the compromises you and your family are willing to make.

For each activity listed on your proposed life portfolio allocation, write down all of the corresponding next steps you can think of. This becomes a checklist of what you know and don't know, as well as a road map for how to proceed in pursuing each of these options. Keep in mind that all options cannot be pursued simultaneously. Prioritizing your plan will determine where you start and what portion of your goals you can realistically pursue at the outset.

As part of revising your goals and developing an action plan, look at the range of possible allocations of your time, and balance one against the other. What combination is going to work for you? And not just in terms of hours allocated. What is the value that you draw from that involvement? What is the contribution that you can make? Are you using your full range of skills? Are you getting the full range of benefits that add up to what you want to get from these involvements, which is a sense of meaning, satisfaction, purpose, continuity, connection, and community?

One way to finalize specifics for your life portfolio plan is to revisit ultimate outcomes and then work backward, step by step. Continue to work back until you find something you can do today, tomorrow, this week, this month, to produce the results. With each goal, ask yourself the following questions: What do I have to do first to accomplish this? What prevents me from having this now, and what can I do to change this? Make sure the plan includes something you can do *today*.

REVISIT, REFLECT, REBALANCE

A final point is that implementing a plan is not a finite process that once completed is over and done (Figure 13.1). A life portfolio involves a complex interplay of parts, like a symphony orchestra. Remove one oboe or violin, and the music starts to sound funny. Alter or eliminate one part of your life portfolio, and the others change to some degree as well. Before you know it, it begins to move off course.

The best way to prevent that is to be proactive and plan ways to maintain, adjust, and rebalance your portfolio long beyond its initial completion. To do that, set up periodic reviews or checkpoints—more frequently initially and less so down the line—to monitor the progress of your portfolio, identify needs for adjustments, and make needed changes. It will also give you the assurance that momentum has not inadvertently carried you in a direction you did not intend to go.

These reviews might simply mean reexamining your life portfolio allocation chart and seeing how closely your current activities

FIGURE 13.1. PLAN-*REFLECT*-REVISE.

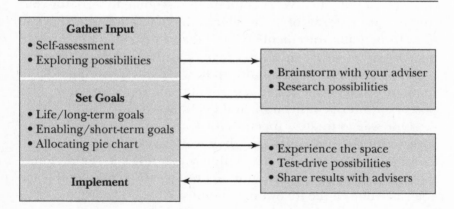

match the original plan. If they diverge but you are satisfied with the current balance, update the allocation chart and use it for your next checkpoint. If the desired balance has been lost, decide what needs to change and make the necessary adjustments.

If you decide on the latter course, take some time to understand how and when a particular allocation or set of activities got off kilter. The content of an involvement may shift, making it less satisfying. Another opportunity may have presented itself. Or external factors may disrupt what otherwise would continue on to a satisfying balance of activities. Whatever the cause, this information can help you remain on the lookout for factors that may steer you off course in the future. This process creates a continual awareness of movement within the portfolio over time.

Yeah, but What Do They *Do* in Portfolio?

When identifying possible pursuits and activities that you can build into your life portfolio, it helps to know what the options are. The following list reflects what some people have chosen to do in their portfolio lifestyles. It is intended to be neither comprehensive nor prescriptive and is offered simply to suggest possibilities you may not have considered.

Employment-Related Options

- *Part-time or interim employment.* Anything less than a full work schedule fits into this category. This could mean one day per week or four days per week. It could involve episodic work that is structured around special projects or needs. It could be full-time work for a period of time followed by time off. It could be tightly scheduled or entirely flexible, depending on your requirements or those of your employer. Whatever the

(Continued)

variation on the theme, this is usually paid work, though it can also entail voluntary work or internships and is characterized by a typical employer-employee relationship (an at-will arrangement, a W-2 position, or employee benefits, to the extent offered by the organization).

• *Consulting.* Consulting takes a range of forms as well. It can be traditional advisory services and related follow-on work, ongoing assistance with special projects, contract work, outsourced activities of various types, and any other arrangement that is based on a 1099 relationship with an organization. In this case, you are self-employed, providing a set of agreed-upon services. Benefits are your responsibility along with any liability related to your contribution, unless you are specifically indemnified through a contractual agreement.

• *Entrepreneurship.* This category includes starting a business, buying a business or franchise, or participating in an early-stage business as an adviser, investor, or part-time leader. In connection with life portfolio, entrepreneurship usually means starting or buying a lifestyle business, that is, one that does not consume as much of one's time as would typically be the case. An intensive start-up phase might be followed by scaled-back requirements or seasonality that permits other involvements. A part-time business can be achieved by employing others to run parts of it, forgoing growth opportunities, deliberately keeping the business small, or selecting a business that offers time off during certain parts of the year. Investing in small or start-up businesses, joining an advisory board, or taking on a part-time leadership position—often preferred during the start-up phase, when capital or other needs may not justify a full-time commitment of resources—are activities that fit naturally into a life portfolio.

• *Board directorships.* Whether you are paid or you volunteer, serving on boards of directors is by definition a part-time endeavor. Regular meetings may be monthly or quarterly, and special meetings, committee work, and other related activities may add up to only a few days per month. This makes more than one board involvement possible, and many clients pursue this as a core part of their life portfolio. Be aware, with not-for-

profit boards, that board service can also lead to other involvements, including fundraising, stepping in when an executive
director or other key employee leaves, helping to conduct a
search for new leadership, and the like. The availability of skills
and time combine to trap many unsuspecting clients into
extended involvements. That may fit your plan well, but it may
also serve to upset the balance you are trying to achieve.

Community Service and Giving Back

- *Civic and nonprofit organizations.* Involvement in civic or
not-for-profit organizations can range from serving on boards or
board committees, taking on leadership roles, providing contract or consulting services or—and let us never forget—rolling
up our sleeves and providing service. Civic groups are governmental, nongovernmental, or advocacy organizations. Not-for-
profit groups may include educational, health care, religious,
cultural, social service, or other community organizations. This
category might also include trade, professional, or industry organizations of various types. Look for fit with your interests but also
transferability of your skills and cultural fit. As mission-driven
organizations, civic and not-for-profit groups often operate differently from other businesses; this can be a source of frustration or challenge for those attempting to transition their
experience into this arena.

- *Philanthropy.* Finding ways to use personal resources or to
raise funds from other sources to advance the mission of social
service and other charitable organizations can be an important
contribution at this stage of life. Family foundations, charitable
trusts, and other such mechanisms are one approach. Less formal but thoughtful contribution strategies, major gifts, and
estate gift plans are options. Other approaches include working with nonprofits to plan events, such as capital appeals and
fundraising events.

- *The international arena.* Professional or humanitarian
interests in an international context can integrate travel into

(Continued)

your portfolio. Humanitarian service includes building homes and schools and other infrastructure projects in undeveloped countries. The Peace Corps and other programs welcome midlife adults as field workers. Nongovernmental organizations may have volunteer as well as paid opportunities for expatriates to apply specialized skills to help needy populations. Escorting travel groups as a guide often involves free travel and accommodations as perks.

Passing on Your Knowledge

- *Coaching, mentoring, advising.* Passing along the benefits of your experience and wisdom to others, particularly younger or less experienced people acquiring more responsibilities, is a satisfying way to contribute to the success of those individuals *and* their organizations. Mentoring can be done informally or in a more structured way, either through organizations that offer such services on a voluntary or paid basis or on boards set up for that purpose.
- *Teaching, writing, speaking.* Another way to convey professional information and insights gleaned from research or years of practical experience is to formalize this knowledge in the form of lectures, classroom instruction, group facilitation, articles, books, white papers, presentations, or panel discussions. For others, there may be an interest in pursuing nonprofessional teaching, writing, or speaking or in taking up these activities in an entirely new context, perhaps returning to an earlier interest, building on an ongoing involvement, or starting fresh to satisfy a new curiosity. Examples might include teaching high school courses, writing poetry or the all-American novel, or lecturing in your areas of interest.
- *Continuing education.* Taking community education classes, auditing college courses, going back to school full-time, or earning a degree in a new area of interest are among the options for those who wish to focus on continued learning. Programs geared specifically to people with flexible schedules but an intense desire to learn are increasingly common. These

are often structured as seminars or discussion groups to allow participatory learning. Some of these involve travel with the benefit of experts who can add an overlay of historical, cultural, or other information on location or during special events. Book groups and other informal education opportunities can also be organized to facilitate continued learning.

Other Pursuits (and Fun)

• *Hobbies and avocations.* Give free reign to long-standing interests, crafts, or any activity you have not been able to enjoy as much as you want. These can be done alone or with others. Consider active ones that get you on your feet, such as gardening, woodworking, birding, pottery, interior design. Build a small fountain in your backyard or a tree house for your grandchildren. But feel free to have fun sitting down reading biographies or novels, doing needlepoint, or drawing. Remember this rule: any activity you engage in for pleasure or relaxation qualifies as a hobby or avocation.

• *Fine arts and performing arts.* You may have long held an interest in or now wish to devote more time to the arts, either as a creator, performer, docent, observer, organizer, collector, or supporter. You may also wish to participate in arts organizations in a leadership, volunteer, fundraising, or board position. Taking lessons, improving skills, playing for enjoyment, joining or starting amateur or professional groups of performing artists, and teaching are all variations on the arts theme.

• *Fitness and sports.* Use your body! Block that boredom! Participating in athletics or coaching not only engages our talent or interest but also helps us stay fit. The boom in master classes in all competitive sports has leveled the playing field for older athletes. Organized leagues and less-formal pickup games offer opportunities as well. Touring stadiums across the country and making the time to attend local sporting events may be options to consider, along with attending the games of grandchildren.

(Continued)

- *Real estate.* Buying and managing residential or commercial properties for an income can involve vocational and avocational components. Building, acquiring, or tending to a second or third home or vacation property can consume a fair amount of time. It can also provide living and investment and relationship options that enrich your life.

- *Travel.* This is an objective that can be achieved in a variety of ways. One is by targeting parts of the country or the world one wishes to explore and then visiting them one by one. Another is to follow a travel theme, planning trips to coincide with festivals, museums, food and wine, or other interests. One might choose to live in various places for extended periods. Cross-continental travel by RV, train, or car is increasingly popular, enabling travelers to see the sights and to experience the life of each community in a more leisurely way. Living in warmer climates during the winter months and returning in summer is another variation on the travel theme. And weekend getaways to nearby points of interest may be more easily scheduled as part of a life portfolio.

CHAPTER FOURTEEN

MOVING INTO PORTFOLIO

We know by now the importance in the creation of a life portfolio of trusting the process, of dealing with feelings, of slowing down and taking the big picture view. That is how we developed our plan. To move forward, however, we must shift gears. This is the part of the journey that takes drive, determination, and a bit of shoe leather.

Now we put our stakes in the ground and get started. If you have a well-thought-out plan, be confident and run with it. Avoid the paralysis of analyzing it beyond a reasonable degree. Remember, "an imperfect plan today is better than a perfect plan tomorrow." You have all the equipment you need. It's time to put on your ten-gallon hat and move on.

If you want to throw open the window and explore possibilities that you might not otherwise be exposed to, you are going to have to get out and talk to new people. You have to open up new territory. Reach beyond your familiar network and interact with new people. You have nothing to lose and everything to gain.

ENTERING NEW TERRITORY

It wouldn't hurt to show some of the chutzpah so evident in a Web log, or blog, on the Internet (www.mymomsblog.blogspot.com). It's the daily work of Millie Garfield, who at age eighty claims to be the oldest blogger in cyberspace. One of her main rules in life, she says, is, "If you don't go out, nothing happens."

A friend discovered the truth of Millie's motto after spending his career in one sector of the banking industry. To liven things up, he made a lateral career move, taking an interim position with a group associated with the Securities and Exchange Commission. He met and formed friendships in entirely new circles of people and interacted on a regular basis with men and women in the U.S. Congress and elsewhere in government. He told me that even though the job was only so-so, the new networks rekindled his curiosity and excitement about life. "I loved the chance to learn new things," he said. He went out, and something happened.

Here's another example. Imagine you have decided you want to open and operate a ferry between the house you just bought on an island in Puget Sound and the Washington mainland. You have done your homework. You have retrieved and analyzed shelved ferry line proposals from governmental or business libraries. You have looked into financing, researched demand, cost, competition, and other issues. Before taking your plan further, ride several ferries in Washington that are vaguely like the one you want to start—not once or twice but many times, on sunny days, in heavy seas, on weekdays and weekends. Talk to other passengers, listen to their conversations, find out what they like and what they don't like about the service. Carry a notebook and write down what you learn. By "going out," you will gain an invaluable perspective. If you decide to go forward, you will probably revise and recommit yourself to your plan.

Woody Allen said, "Eighty percent of life is showing up." Show up at places like conventions, lectures, trade shows, and seminars. Talk to new people at every event. I have had countless clients whose attendance at events and classes has led directly to portfolio opportunities. One such client happened to sit on a panel with someone to whom he had previously sent his résumé. By meeting and getting to know the contact in person, our client eventually landed an opportunity at his co-panelist's company.

INVESTING IN YOURSELF

It's critical as you move forward to be internally invested in seeing your plan through. This is putting stakes in the ground. Even small steps can build your sense of ownership and determination. Let nothing stop you. "Is there any law that prevents me from declaring Pelican Island a National Bird Sanctuary?" asked Franklin D. Roosevelt. "Very well, then, I do declare it."

One thing that can stop us is fear that our timing is off. Hundreds of people have expressed some perfectly good idea or goal to me and then said, "But you know, it's really too late to get started on that one." I remind them of the story President John F. Kennedy told at a 1963 tree planting. French Marshal Louis Lyautey asked his gardener to plant a tree. The worker objected that the slow-growing tree would take a century to reach maturity. "In that case," said the marshal, "there is no time to lose. Plant it this afternoon."

Don't be afraid to push the envelope. When you write letters and network around a particular allocation goal, give the presentation all you have. Tell the world, this idea is *of the moment* for me; it's my call, my duty, to develop it. Now is not the time to be diplomatic or wonder what others will think of your moves. This is your chance to pursue your life and your legacy the way you want. So just be honest, open, and simple. Lock on to your talents, and your instincts will guide you forward.

As pieces of your portfolio plan fall in place, you may find yourself all worked up and going at it like a twenty-year-old. If so, there is no need to chastise yourself that you failed the portfolio rule of balance. Yes, I promote balance and believe in it. But when we get "in the zone" of what we want to do with our lives, we may hit a pocket of PEPC that puts us into overdrive. There is nothing wrong with that, for a limited period of time. It may seem self-serving, but intense concentration is sometimes needed to succeed in this very important and personal path. Writing a book can be an unbalanced zone. It was for me.

NETWORKING

Networking is the single most effective way to achieve your portfolio goals. It's not, however, the easiest way. Successful networking may take months of persistent phoning, letter writing, and meetings. You will have to leave voice messages, send e-mails, request meetings or follow-ups, and be able to tolerate not hearing back. Some days, it will feel more like seeding a large empty field than reaping the benefits of your efforts. But it will pay off.

Networking is ultimately about building relationships of respect, trust, listening, and empathy. It's not unlike developing friendships. We actually invest time, energy, and genuine caring in our personal and professional support networks. Those in whom we make these investments may prove invaluable at some point. You get out what you put in.

Networking is about drawing on deep connections built up and nurtured over a lifetime. What is important is not the *quantity* of your contacts—how big your Rolodex is—but rather the *quality* of your contacts. High-quality relationships to which you turn over time are among your greatest resources. Your mind-set should be this: you are important to me, and I may be important to you.

Networking should not be a chore. It's really about being a good person. Start by being a contact yourself, sharing what you know, doing favors, helping and taking an interest in others and their needs. Do this routinely, automatically, as a habit of mind, and that may break the natural tendency to think there has to be a payback. As we have seen, the paradox is that in the long run helping others may be the most selfish thing you can do.

A recent portfolio client, Jeffrey Smith, says that networking helped him keep abreast of change in his industry, which contributed to his landing a portfolio opportunity: "As I was networking, I developed an appreciation for the new trends and innovation in my industry more than I had before, and I feel as though it made me an expert," he says. "Better equipped, I networked with the founder of a business whom I had met ten years ago, and through our discussions it appeared that they had a need and I was a good match to fulfill it."

SELLING YOUR PLAN TO OTHERS

Selling yourself is required to develop opportunities that create satisfying portfolio lifestyles. Desirable life and work opportunities usually go to people with the best sales and marketing skills—regardless of whether they are the most qualified. What that statement lacks in fairness it makes up for in accuracy. There are no shortcuts; there are no high-tech ways to streamline the process; there are no alternatives to sending letters and e-mails, picking up the phone, having meetings, and following up. The ability to make the sale is the universal *must*. As in any business enterprise, selling is unavoidable. If you want to avoid another grueling full-time career, or a full-time do-nothing retirement, accept that you must sell yourself. It's worth the effort; your port-folio stage in life may last forty years.

In the context of putting a portfolio plan into action, selling means presenting, promoting, marketing, making known, and gen-erating interest and excitement in what you have to offer and what you want to do. The easy part is doing this among those we already know. We have to work harder at "selling" ourselves in wider cir-cles of people. But the further out the ripples of interest carry, the more likely we are to realize opportunities and elements that together create a rewarding life portfolio.

"But I'm not a natural salesperson," you say. "I *hate* selling. I'm the world's worst marketer!" I hear that all the time. I understand, and I sympathize with people who tell me that. And my response is usually the same: find a mission—you'll do just fine selling it. After you identify your passion, it will be easy to assume the stance, the posture, of a salesperson.

Here are some ideas to get you started:

- *Research the customer.* Get to know all you can about the *customer*—any person you meet who potentially holds the key to your portfo-lio opportunity. Research that person's life situation, motivations, education, hobbies, and philanthropic interests. Discover what you have in common. This is critical: before you meet, write down any-thing you have learned about the needs, goals, financial issues, industry or knowledge trends, or competitive challenges faced by the person, company, group, or nonprofit organization.
- *Offer solutions.* Focus on solving *their* needs—not yours. Instead of saying, "I want . . ." or "I need . . ." ask, "How can I help *you?*" By being a problem solver, you will illustrate the value of your experi-ence and knowledge.
- *Practice the "elevator drill."* When you are asked what you want, you have to be able to answer quickly and succinctly. I call this an elevator drill, because you should be able to get your point across in the thirty seconds or so that an average elevator ride takes. Per-fect your thirty-second story: who you are, where you came from, where you're going, why you're qualified, and how they can help you. In other words, craft your sales pitch.
- *Engage all your senses.* Sometimes the *way* you present has more impact than the message—the words themselves. Help your

contact visualize by creating vivid mental images that ask him or her to *imagine*. Be animated and positive, and your enthusiasm will come across.

- *Practice the Columbo Factor.* Curiosity is a huge part of this process. Ask lots of questions. We encourage what we call "the Columbo Factor." Just like that disheveled police detective from the TV show of the same name, ask the question that makes the difference. "I want to ask one more question," he would say. That last "gotcha" question might be the one that finalizes the opportunity.

- *Compartmentalize.* Don't take rejections personally; you must put emotional distance between yourself and the situation. I know this is hard—especially if you are not used to hearing no. But even the best ideas are rejected occasionally.

- *Write a press release about yourself.* At New Directions, the challenge of writing a press release explaining clearly the nature, purpose, and form of a new initiative can be worth more to us than the use that is made of it. It forces us to think clearly and precisely about what we are saying or trying to do. The result is greater inner clarity. People implementing portfolio plans can benefit from a similar method. So get your press kit ready. This exercise increases our ownership in what we are trying to do and so hastens the transition from employee to self-employed, independent contractor, and entrepreneur—a process required for creating portfolios.

- *Personal publicity.* Don't forget to conduct your own publicity. Write and publish articles and commentaries. Teach a class or seminar. Create your own Web page, if you have not already done so, or start a blog. Consult, serve on panels, and do public speaking. All these will give you a competitive edge.

- *Sell features and benefits.* Features are your skills, and they are easy to communicate. As a result, many people forget to talk about how their features will "benefit" the customer. At New Directions, we say it like this: sell *news* not newspapers; sell *vision* not glasses. News and vision are the benefits, newspapers and glasses, the features.

- *Phone skills.* Making phone calls is part of the process of creating portfolios. Set up the calls as telephone interviews, which will allow you to cover many contacts in a short time. Set a goal for how many calls you are going to make each day. But don't expect a response better than *2 percent*. It may take hundreds of calls to get a handful of positive responses, but the more calls you make, the more yes's you will get. Stand and pace when calling.

• *Form a team.* Recruiting a personal sales force will greatly increase your networking reach. Select a group of friends and colleagues and stay in close touch. You might start with your personal board of advisers, which I introduced in Chapter Five and further developed in Chapter Nine. Involve your spouse or partner and family when appropriate. Ask the group to meet on a regular basis and delegate as much as possible. Ask for introductions, referrals, and leads to potential portfolios. But remember, it's a team. You all help one another.

CLOSING THE DEAL

How do we bring closure to our portfolio plans? It certainly takes persistence. But it also takes negotiation skills. Because most portfolio situations must be created and developed, every step of the way will require give-and-take, compromises, trade-offs, and concessions. In their book *Getting to Yes* (1991, pp. 4–5), Roger Fisher and William Ury advise readers to be flexible: "Arguing over positions produces unwise and inefficient agreements," they write. "The more you try to convince the other side of the impossibility of changing your opening position, the more difficult it becomes to do so." So keep an open mind.

Selling yourself doesn't always come easy, but no portfolio opportunity will come without it. Hockey legend Wayne Gretzky's useful advice could be applied to those looking to land portfolio opportunities. "You miss 100 percent of the shots you never take."

CHAPTER FIFTEEN

POCKETS OF TURBULENCE

A high-ranking officer, under the command of General Norman Schwarzkopf Jr. during and after the 1990–1991 Gulf War, retired several years ago. A career Army man, he had been used to fast-paced action, on the battlefield and across his desk. "After I retired from the military," he told our portfolio clients, "I thought the phone would never stop ringing. I was wrong. It went dead in less than a month."

Welcome to retirement. Thinning calendars. Days that can feel like a train ride across Siberia. An e-mail in-box that makes you wonder if your computer is really connected to the Internet. (You find out it is.) Guilt over not being productive. Fear of making a mistake that you may not have years enough to correct. A spouse who keeps asking you to walk the dog or go on an errand, any errand, outside the house.

A life that feels unhinged.

Yes, this is a bit of a caricature, and people taking more exciting postcareer and portfolio paths may be amused. But I have some strong advice for even these people: don't kid yourself. What you are doing differs from the old version, yes, but you will face—and have to make adjustments for—some of the same psychological and emotional challenges and upheaval in your life infrastructure.

Of course, people vary widely in how much change-related stress they experience and how they react to it. Moving into a portfolio lifestyle is harder for some individuals and easier for others. But there are pockets of turbulence that we have repeatedly heard about from clients in the dozen years that we have offered our Life Portfolio Program. I call these portfolio aftershocks *minefields*. Here

I will look at some of the main ones and offer suggestions for defusing them.

Separating from something that has been a part of one's personal infrastructure for a long time can cause a person to come unglued. Now the old titles, status, support systems, and many work relationships are gone. Not preparing for the reality of this change will prevent you from moving forward smoothly into a portfolio lifestyle.

Take time for closure. You may be doing new things and forging new relationships. But the fact is that your old relationships with many people have changed. Not dealing with this can make you feel rejected unnecessarily. A complaint we often hear, especially from executives accustomed to being at the center of things, is, "Why didn't they ask my opinion before they did that?" Or, "Nobody asks my advice anymore." These thoughts drag you down. If you stop hearing from your former office, don't assume it is because you were not valued. Their behavior is normal and appropriate, not a referendum on you. And even if it were, what others think of us does not set our value as human beings anyway.

How to deal with the change in your status? Build your new networks long before you leave. Find new circles, discover new colleagues. Turn for support and connection to your family and old friends and to new friends and new work associates. Be too engaged to care.

There is also the loss of schedules and routines to structure time. Many clients who enter the less-structured portfolio mode have difficulty managing their time. Again, it's the hardest for those not used to doing it. They had secretaries, assistants, and various technological aids to keep them on track during their days and weeks. They lack the discipline and the support staff needed to get through the day seamlessly. "I have no one to delegate to," one client said. "It drives me crazy when I have to replace the ink cartridge in my printer or make my own travel arrangements. My job has always been to solve complex global problems. How do I handle the ink problem?"

In portfolio, you may have to develop these skills. You are self-employed now! It's up to you to use your time wisely, and that may include performing the support functions that enable you to exercise your special skills. You have to set goals and stick with them, but you may need to change the ink cartridge, too!

An important mind-clearing strategy is to *reject demands on your time that don't fit with your overall goals.* Failing to do this can turn purpose into mere busyness. Retired people often say they are too busy to be bored, and a few have told me that they have never been so busy in their lives. But there's a big difference between being busy and being purposefully engaged, doing things that satisfy us and help us to learn and to grow as human beings. As one portfolio client told another in one of our seminars, and only half-jokingly, "You have to be careful or this portfolio thing could turn into real work."

Ellen Graham, a writer involved in several causes and community boards and projects, said in an article in the *Wall Street Journal* (December 16, 2002) that her life only *looked* interesting and well structured on the outside. "Inwardly, I'm as scattered and unfocused as a 16-year-old, and I suspect I'm not alone." The same questions keep rising to the surface: Am I busy simply for the sake of being busy? And how did I get swept up in a bunch of activities that to be honest don't excite me all that much?

So if you are an architect and you are asked to chair the condo association's sidewalk improvement committee, do like Nancy Reagan and "just say no!" If you do, you'll stay on track, getting involved only in those things that are moving you closer to your goals. The resulting satisfaction should be strong enough to help you overcome troublesome steps along the way.

The problem, of course, is that we *want* to do many things, and further, these may be good and worthwhile things in and of themselves, such as working for nonprofits, charities, or humanitarian organizations. This is a dilemma that we should anticipate and think about during the planning process, which is why I am so emphatic about its importance. It helps us confront the challenge in portfolio of finding the right balance between, on the one hand, structure, purpose, and meaningful involvements and, on the other hand, flexibility that leaves us in control of our time. This was exactly the nut portfolio client Bill Coleman had to crack, and he readily admits he did not do it right. Bill asked me to share his story as a heads-up to others.

Bill Coleman is a can-do guy with a sterling résumé. In the private sector, he was chief executive officer at Hancock Natural Resource Group, cofounder and president of an airport mall development firm, and a managing director at a Wall Street investment house. In the public sector, he was chief of aviation for the Massachusetts Port Authority, budget director of the Massachusetts Department of Human Services, and a consultant on health and aviation to the federal government.

Bill began his life portfolio at age sixty-two and planned to work in the nonprofit arena. He was passionate about environmental issues and convinced that *market-based environmentalism* was more effective than the confrontational approach of activists. Bill was also excited by the thought that he could bring his extensive business background to this arena. He was recruited by a superb nonprofit organization and took a senior position that was a bit more of a job than he really wanted.

What Bill did not reckon with, he says, is the "hand-to-mouth financial nature" of nonprofits and nongovernmental organizations. "Because of competition for funding, doing good work is not enough. They have to find a niche in their area and aggressively defend it." The financial stress on the organization and emphasis on fundraising were greater than he anticipated. In reality, he said, the job actually made his work-life balance worse than it had been in his prior position. "I am giving the job 140 percent, working like a 40-year-old," he wrote to me in a letter. "I'm dealing with it because of my commitment to environmental issues. But it doesn't make any sense."

Demands on your time that upset the applecart are one of the major minefields to watch out for in portfolio.

However the opposite problem—empty time—can make you feel guilty. That, too, is a problem. "I wanted to watch *The Battle of Midway, Part I,* on the History Channel," a former executive who chose a portfolio lifestyle told me. "But it was on at three in the afternoon and I just felt guilty. What am I doing watching TV in the middle of the afternoon? I got over it though, and I enjoyed it so much that I watched *Part II* the next day."

"I have this nagging thing about not working," another client confided. "Am I cheating my family by not making more of my earning years?"

A deeper problem that can trouble people who separate from long careers is a perceived loss of identity. The mistake many of us make is to allow ourselves to be defined by our careers. That may seem to work for a while. But as I have been saying throughout this book, careers are only one portion of our entire lives, and not necessarily the largest portion. If we fail to diversify, we pay the price when the props are pulled away. One client, a woman who led a manufacturing company, hit this pocket of turbulence. "I had to get over the cocktail-party embarrassment of not being able to define myself by my career," she told me. She recognized that it's a whole new ball game with whole new rules.

In reality, of course, we don't lose our identity when we quit a career. We may lose *that* identity or *an* identity, but not our whole identity. It's better to think of one's identity as *changing*, which is what the portfolio mind-set is about. It can be similar to the struggle that young adults face. And in truth it is healthy, because it forces us to ask questions we thought we had answered. Who am I? Do I matter? There can be a sense of loss of purpose, experts say, when the underpinnings of the old situation are removed and no new ones are in place. Be sure you have new ones ready.

Navigating Marital Stress

One of the largest potential pockets of turbulence is the realm of our intimate relationships. Some stress and dislocation is inevitable on the home front. By being open about our feelings,

"I had planned to step down to spend more time with my family, but my family talked me out of it."

Source: By Bunny Hoest, copyright 2006, published in *Parade* magazine.

adaptive, and respectful of the needs of others, these can generally be minimized.

Strain in marital relationships may begin soon. When a partner who has long worked outside the home starts to work at home, as is frequently the case, tensions can increase.

"My wife has three phone lines in the house," wrote a client. "One is for the Internet, one is for her real estate business, and one is for personal calls. I sit in my space at home and wait for the little red light on the phone to go off so I can quickly pick up and make my own calls. Too many times, she beats me to it."

One man spoke at our Life Portfolio Program after a distinguished business career that included many years as the chief executive of a large financial institution. He decided to work on his portfolio projects in an office on the second floor of his house. It happened to share a wall with his wife's office. As he sat in deep thought, he could hear her move about. He could hear her telephone ring and fax machine beep, and he could hear her conversations. After a week of this, he began to think that he could hear her computer keyboard. That is when he decided he would go crazy if he did not work outside his house, he told me.

A life portfolio is about what matters to you. That means it features the involvement and preferences of those you love most. That is why we strongly encourage the participation of families in the assessment and planning processes. Nevertheless, spouses have their own lives to live, and for women, this increasingly means managing their own careers. One partner continuing to work full-time after the other has retired can be a combustible situation.

When women entered the workforce in massive numbers over the last thirty years, the majority did so not after their education, as I've reported, but when they were between the ages of thirty-five and fifty. Having begun their careers later, these women are often on an entirely different time track than the typical male. They are not ready to leave their careers behind. "We're dealing with a stage of the marriage relationship that's occurring for the first time in history," says sociologist Phyllis Moen. (Moen was quoted in a *New York Times* story on March 23, 2004, headlined, "He's Retired, She's Working, They're Not Happy.") Tensions can escalate when one partner is ready for a long-awaited and well-deserved break and the other still wants or needs to put in long hours at the office. Or one partner wants to reorganize his or her life around new priorities and the other is not ready to leave the old ones.

"When I found out I was retiring before I had planned, I kept telling my wife about my retirement program," one client told me. "Finally, she said, 'Let me tell you about *my* retirement program.' "

When neither partner works full-time, and both are around the house with flexible or open schedules, a different set of problems arises. Renee Solomon is a retired Columbia University sociologist who now counsels couples coping with retirement-related concerns. "Marriages can be put on the rocks when two people are thrust together with so much time," she says. "Be aware of the discomfort; it doesn't mean you need a divorce."

Just because prior commitments required separation from your spouse much of the week does *not* mean that with those commitments gone you want to spend every waking minute together. Talk about this openly beforehand. Figure out how much time you need alone. Decide which regular activities will be done jointly and which separately.

Failure to do so can make a long commute to work start to look good again. The wife of one client blasted this off to me: "A retired husband is a wife's full-time job." Another wife sent me an e-mail that pleaded, "Get my husband out of the kitchen! He's rearranging my spice rack."

Remember that there is no rule that spouses and partners must share the same interests and motivations. They have their own ideas on how to spend their time, where to locate, lifestyle choices, and the like. Compromise is an important part of maintaining a healthy relationship. Recognize that the need to find middle ground when your choices conflict, along with the need to amend your own plans accordingly, is an important reality in living a successful life portfolio.

AVOIDING ISOLATION

Isolation is also a big problem. Studies of people living alone without a sense of community indicate that isolation undermines the will to live and that death often follows prolonged social isolation. Isolation can lead to depression, which is more frequent among older adults.

A "Ten" on the Emotional Richter Scale

A former CEO of a major financial services company retired
and found it extremely challenging. With his permission, I am
sharing excerpts from a letter he wrote me so that others
who have similar feelings will know they are not alone. The
excerpts have been altered to conceal the person's identity.

It's been the biggest adjustment in my life—including getting divorced, moving between jobs or cities, even experiencing the death of a child. This has been a ten on the
Richter Scale of adjustments.

Before retiring, I felt prepared. I thought I had done
a lot of work on my next phase. But I realize I wasn't
ready. I've really struggled about what I should do next.
So in spite of all the work I've done, I give myself a C+
on retirement.

I've been alone a lot. That's been hard on me
because of my makeup. I'm a people person, used to
having a lot of outside activities. Now I do stuff alone.
That's a major change. I've experienced a loss of daily
achievements and of being part of a team.

If I had all the money in the world, I wouldn't be
happy if I didn't have a sense of achievement. When
I told my daughter I was going to do this, retire that is,
she said, "I hope you don't get depressed." I guess she
knows me!

What I've gone through is probably what many go
through. You get a lot of stroking when you have a career,
and you lose it when you leave.

"I still have lots of ideas," one client told me, "but there is no
one to tell them to."

I may be old fashioned, but I think the boom in Internet-
connected home offices that modern technology has driven is contributing to this problem. Telecommuting and working at home
have their obvious strong points, but one of the dangers is not having the face time with others.

Throughout the book, I have stressed the importance of balance in portfolio, how to find it and how to maintain it. I encourage the mosaic approach to portfolio because I know that it creates a more dynamic whole. But I encourage you to be mindful of the tension between pursuing a combination of activities and having a central theme or structure that grounds your life portfolio. "I like the portfolio life, but everything is kind of interim and temporary," said another client. "I wish I had one activity that was longer term." That in fact is an excellent idea. I encourage portfolio clients to choose one of their activities or allocations as the anchor—the glue—of their life portfolio, at least for a set period of time, after which they may wish to reevaluate.

The biggest problem is one I have already addressed, but it bears repeating. The people who without question have the toughest time—and who may come to me as a result of this—are those who did not plan. Sadly, they may not have even realized that they were failing to plan because they expected retirement to evolve by itself. They were deluded into thinking that rest, leisure, and recreation would be enough. They simply did not give it enough thought, and they are the people most at risk of being bored and without a purpose.

I want to make a final comment about a minefield that will never ever be cleared. Longevity has its limits. There will never be a masters swimming competition for thousand-year-olds. Or at least I hope not! Whatever path we take in extended middle age and beyond, we must accept our mortality. As they reach retirement age, some individuals truly face this for the first time. Perhaps they have been too busy, but now they see that their time on earth is limited. As this sinks in, try saying to yourself, "I'm lucky, today and every day I'm alive. I still have time to get things done, to enjoy the gift of life, and to do something with it, to make a significant contribution." I say that is great news! It *really is* never too late. Find a passion. Live that passion. It may push mortality off further than you think.

I pointed out these minefields not because I can solve them but in the hope that those for whom they resonate will begin to talk to others with similar concerns and others who may know better how to cope. I offer them in hope that people will feel validated. Feeling validated may inspire us to begin these conversations with others and thus find ways to cope.

Beyond that, I urge you to take it slow, if need be, and remember to introduce change into your life bit by bit, weaning yourself off old activities as you go. Challenge "facts" and habits. See life as new each and every day. Be grateful for it. Find ways to stay energized and optimistic, because all the evidence shows that such an attitude can make a difference.

I will close this chapter with the wisdom of Winston Churchill, who said it all on the topic of life's troublesome toils and tests. This is a thought we should carve inside our brains and repeat when the challenge of change gets to be too much.

His advice is, "If you are going through hell, *keep going.*"

CHAPTER SIXTEEN

THE GOAL BEYOND

Grow old along with me!
The best is yet to be,
The last of life, for which the first was made.

—ROBERT BROWNING

The portfolio perspective on life is much about being happy. That may sound simplistic to some, but in my view, it comes down to that. Finding and doing what gives us fulfillment should be our ultimate goal. I really believe this, and so I was glad to learn that William James thought so as well. For most people, "How to gain, how to keep, how to recover happiness," he said, is "the secret motive for what they do" (1994, p. 77). I don't mean pleasure or self-satisfaction, or the feeling of being "up" or at the top of our game, although those things are good in themselves.

I mean the intangible sense of well-being that comes from knowing that you are living the life you have been given, that you have contributed something to the world, and that to the best of your ability you are realizing your unique gifts. The Japanese have a word for this, *ikigai*, which translates to finding significance and purpose in later life. By happy, I mean the answer that emerged from a 2004 study, "The Future of Retirement," sponsored by the global bank HSBC. When eleven thousand people in ten countries were asked what contributed most to achieving a happy old age, the vast majority chose "loving family and friends."

Life after fifty is a time when people who have not already done so accept that enduring happiness does not come from financial success alone. The absence of money can drive us crazy, yet having it does not automatically mean we will be happy. It does not take money to be in what psychologists call the state of *flow*, or complete absorption in a task to the extent that we lose track of time. You can spend a fortune on a yacht or luxury vacation or fancy car and not get a lot of flow from it. Or you can be in that state without spending a nickel by gardening, hanging out with your grandchildren, or building model ships.

The actual form our happiness takes does not really matter. It could mean being a lawyer, a parent, a teacher, a manager, or a street sweeper who takes pride in what he does. A remark attributed to Bertrand Russell expresses it well: "Anything you're good at contributes to happiness."

Jack Wilson, a New Directions colleague who lives in Hilton Head, told of greeting a newcomer there. Jack said that when he asked the man what he did for a living, he replied, "I'm a tax adviser much of the time. But when I'm at my best, I'm a banjo player."

I know that what Russell said is true, but I also wrestle with this. "Follow your bliss" can sound irresponsible or self-serving. If we serve ourselves, one might well ask, does that mean that we are *not* serving others? My answer is this: not necessarily. I find that those who connect to their deep resources and joy are more able and likely to help others. Surveys prove this. I have recently started to think that if happiness can be pragmatically shown to make the world a better place, if it can be rationally promoted as an incentive to giving, then maybe we should teach it and preach it more, have courses on it, set it out before young people as a life destination.

At the very same time, however, we have to be careful about treating happiness as if it were some kind of separate entity or isolated quality. It is not easily pursued as a goal in and of itself. Many of my own experiences of happiness come from being connected to others, sometimes being valued by others, even doing small things for others, like leaving the person who cleans hotel rooms or a taxi driver an oversized tip, or a two-second pause to make friendly eye contact with the turnpike toll collector. I have been privileged over the last twenty years to work with a number of passionate people. They have inspired others and me. One of my great sources of happiness is that I have possibly made a bit of difference in their lives. So in a way, my happiness is a by-product of interactions that are larger than me.

Happiness is a conundrum. How, for example, do I explain to clients that volunteering as a job coach or mentor to homeless veterans or low-income people will make them happy? It tends to come out that if you do this (serve others), it will make you happy. But that does not fully explain scientific research that shows that when people feel happy—that is, when they are in a state of happiness—they are then more willing to help others. A team of University of California psychologists reviewed hundreds of studies over decades and found that "chronically happy" people are more successful in life and work. Their emotional state tends to make them confident, optimistic, and energetic—which also makes them more likable, increasing the chance of positive social connections. Sonja Lyubomirsky, lead author of the study, said past research has assumed a causal link: success leads to happiness. But her team found that this is not always true. A positive, happy outlook, she wrote, "can lead to success-oriented behaviors."

I cannot untangle all these complexities, but I do know one thing. It is striking how many people tell me that they are unsatisfied, unfulfilled, or unhappy. I sometimes meet with clients who have a blank expression on their faces when I ask what makes them happy. "I'm not sure what happy means," they say. Or, "Does it matter?" they ask.

One of them told me:

> I've been so programmed to look at happiness as exceeding quota, making my numbers, pleasing customers, cutting overhead, and as a result of all that, hoping the stock will go up. Now those clear measures are gone. I don't have a scorecard for being happy anymore. Where do I start?

Opinion research confirms that unhappiness is widespread. Surveys consistently show that about two out of three American workers are dissatisfied with their jobs. A broad survey conducted by the respected National Opinion Research Center found that the number of Americans reporting at least one major life problem edged up slightly—from 88 to 92 percent—from 1991 through 2004. Life spans have lengthened, prosperity and living standards have risen, but we seem increasingly torn by doubts about the quality of our lives. Those doubts are not only more widespread but seem to arise at an earlier age than ever. Maybe it is a positive sign that Generation X'ers and Y'ers are questioning received wisdom and looking for new paths. And perhaps rising doubt is explained by the fact that having mostly met our basic needs for food and shelter, we are more focused on the issue of personal fulfillment. Whatever the answer, the fact that the American drive toward greater material comfort and affluence has produced so much unhappiness is another paradox of happiness.

A phrase that resonates in my mind is the *pursuit of happiness*. This term, maybe this whole idea, has uniquely American roots. Thomas Jefferson put it in the second sentence of the Declaration of Independence. All persons "are endowed by their Creator with certain unalienable Rights, that among these are Life, Liberty and the pursuit of Happiness." What did Jefferson mean? For starters, it had nothing to do with owning a Mercedes, getting a piece of some start-up's initial public offering, or having a house larger than an aircraft carrier.

I have always had a great interest in American history, and not just about politics and major movements but the stories of how people lived their lives. When I read about the people of that era, I know that signature phrase must have meant something beyond acquiring things. Back then, it was a radical idea that people should get to decide for themselves what they wanted to do with their lives, what had meaning and value, and what was thus worth pursuing. That was the job of the king or the church. So what did they pursue? Money, of course, and why not? But money was only one of the things Americans wanted back then. They had commitments to one another, to their religious beliefs, to their ideas and ideals about honesty, thrift, service, and caring for others.

I am afraid that the "pursuit of happiness" that most comes to mind today is but a cheap knockoff of the real thing. Accepting the ersatz "he-who-dies-with-the-most-toys-wins" version of this Jeffersonian dream has not made too many people happy. I have learned that again and again. Discovering misplaced priorities or shallow goals can be a disturbing thing for people past fifty years of age. But that is only the bad news. The good news is that the period in life that we used to call *retirement* is an opportunity to find out what really makes us happy. Tom Hagan of Covington, Ohio, found out. When Hagan turned fifty-six, he sold his own pharmacy business and took a different job within his industry that paid less but demanded fewer hours and gave fewer headaches. "The secret to life is being fulfilled," he told an interviewer for the local newspaper. "It has nothing to do with money. I have friends who are worth $50 million who are miserable. I love my life. I'm still working, and I plan to work until I die."

Clients pursuing the portfolio path have told me similar things. Their words suggest that the rainbow of life may have a pot of gold on the far end if we look for it. "To me, happiness is the satisfaction from giving back, mentoring," said one portfolio client who volunteered for us.

I believe in the link between a sense of purpose and happiness. However, I recognize that there is no surefire recipe. Happiness may come in stages, first as one awareness or experience, then as another. When people begin to live out their life portfolio, happiness may arrive as a feeling of release. That is how a former partner at a Chicago law firm described it to me.

"I'm happy now that I've got my feet comfortably planted in midair!" he said. "No meetings, no joining in the conference room. The knot in my stomach's gone. I love walking around without it. It's liberating. I walk by meeting rooms filled with lawyers and I could care less what's going on!"

If we channel this exuberance into pursuits, other paths to happiness will appear when the novelty of freedom wears off.

What makes me happy? I have always loved setting and meeting goals. Crossing off items on my "to do" lists makes me happy. Done. An accomplishment! I get happiness from giving people good news. Increasingly, and maybe this is part of my own portfolio awakenings, happiness is not rushing as much. Focusing line by line when I enjoy a book rather than scanning it for points. Paying attention to people and details I have missed at another time in my life. Not always climbing the mountain. Trying to be fulfilled by reaching small goals along the way.

OUR NEGLECTED CALLINGS

Charles Francis Potter (1882–1965) was a minister and Bible scholar who wrote a book addressed to older people called *Technique of Happiness* (1935). At the time, people thought nothing of describing someone of sixty years of age as "elderly," and Potter does so. That might tempt a reader today to slam the book shut. But if we grant the difference in longevity then and continue reading, we find that the minister has more to say.

Potter calls finding an outlet through which to express our true selves "the field to cultivate for later happiness." People in their sixties are often disappointed that a quick review "reveals no one great thing done" in their lives, he writes. But the man who "takes inventory and devotes himself for weeks and months to self-examination [which I call assessment] may discover some neglected element which, when brought into its proper place, may transform his life" and reveal his true calling.

> Some desire in boyhood that got buried because of other interests may suddenly appear again. It may prove to have been his true bent, his real calling, and even the man of sixty, perhaps especially the man of sixty, ripened and strengthened by life experience, may take this boyhood ambition and in a surprisingly short time find himself doing more with the thing than he could have as a boy [Potter, 1935, p. 201].

That passage concludes, "We have many second chances in life, sometimes even tenth chances." I was thrilled to read that, because life portfolios are really about chances two through ten—and beyond.

I have talked a lot about happiness but have not given much advice, so allow me to close with some. Do not chase happiness. The success of a chase can usually be seen afterward fairly quickly. We got what we sought, or we did not. But with happiness, we sometimes do not know we have it until much later. So rushing at it will not work. Pursue other worthwhile goals, and let happiness come to you. Look for new opportunities to apply or refine what you do best. Tackle challenges that are meaningful to your life and your age now. Jonas Salk, who invented the polio vaccine, was once asked what his main goal in life was. Salk replied, "to become a good ancestor." That's a goal worthy of portfolio or any stage of life, one that almost surely leads to happiness. It is not an easy one, but creating and living out your own *life portfolio* might be a meaningful way to start.

ED BOOKS

Message. New York: Doubleday, 1989.
Old Tappan, N.J.: Macmillan, 1970.
se of Life's Changes. Reading, Mass:

First, Break All the Rules. New York:

hambhala, 2004.
rica's Moral Crisis. New York: Simon

kening Human Potential in the Second
000.

Crowley, C., and Lodge, H. S. *Younger Next Year: A Guide to Living Like 50 Until You're 80 and Beyond.* New York: Workman, 2004.

De Puy, W. H. *Threescore Years and Beyond; or Experiences of the Aged.* New York: Phillips & Hunt, 1871.

Dychtwald, K. *Age Power: How the 21st Century Will Be Ruled by the New Old.* New York: Tarcher/Putnam, 1999.

Dychtwald, K., and Kadlec, D. J. *The Power Years.* New York: Wiley, 2005.

Dyer, W. W. *Inspiration: Your Ultimate Calling.* Carlsbad, Calif.: Hay House, 2006.

Eisenberg, L. *The Number: A Completely Different Way to Think About the Rest of Your Life.* Waterville, Maine: Thorndike Press, 2006.

Erikson, E. H. *Identity and the Life Cycle.* New York: Norton, 1980.

Everett, M. *Making a Living While Making a Difference: The Expanded Guide to Creating Careers with a Conscience.* Gabriola Island, B.C.: New Society, 1999.

Fisher, R., and Ury, W. *Getting to Yes: Negotiating Agreement Without Giving In.* New York: Penguin Books, 1991.

Freedman, M. *Prime Time: How Baby Boomers Will Revolutionize Retirement and Transform America.* New York: Public Affairs, 1999.

Freudenheim, E. *Looking Forward: An Optimist's Guide to Retirement.* New York: Stewart, Tabori and Chang, 2004.

Friedman, T. L. *The World Is Flat: A Brief History of the Twenty-First Century.* New York: Farrar, Straus & Giroux, 2005.

Garis, H. R. *Uncle Wiggily's Story Book.* New York: Platt & Munk, 1987.

Gladwell, M. *The Tipping Point: How Little Things Can Make a Big Difference.* New York: Little, Brown, 2000.

Hardin, P. P. *What Are You Doing with the Rest of Your Life?* San Rafael, Calif.: New World Library, 1992.

His Holiness the Dalai Lama, and Cutler, H. C. *The Art of Happiness.* New York: Riverhead Books, 1998.

Honoré, C. *In Praise of Slowness: How a Worldwide Movement Is Challenging the Cult of Speed.* San Francisco: HarperSanFrancisco, 2004.

Hudson, F. M., and McLean, P. D. *LifeLaunch: A Passionate Guide to the Rest of Your Life.* Santa Barbara, Calif.: Hudson Press, 2000.

Ibarra, H. *Working Identity.* Boston: Harvard Business School Press, 2003.

Johnson, S. *Who Moved My Cheese?* New York: Putnam, 1998.

Kinder, G. *The Seven Stages of Money Maturity.* New York: Delacorte Press, 1999.

Leider, R., and Shapiro, D. A. *Repacking Your Bags: Lighten Your Load for the Rest of Your Life.* San Francisco: Berrett-Koehler, 2002.

Levine, S. B. *Inventing the Rest of Our Lives: Women in Second Adulthood.* New York: Viking Penguin, 2005.

Myers, D. G. *The Pursuit of Happiness.* New York: Morrow, 1992.

Osteen, J. *Your Best Life Now: 7 Steps to Living at Your Full Potential.* New York: Warner Books, 2004.

Perls, T. T., and Silver, M. H. *Living to 100.* New York: Basic Books, 1999.

Pink, D. *Free Agent Nation.* New York: Warner Books, 2001.

Pink, D. *A Whole New Mind.* New York: Riverhead Books, 2005.

Pollan, S. M., and Levine, M. *Second Acts.* New York: HarperResource, 2003.

Raynolds, J. *The Halo Effect: How Volunteering Can Lead to a More Fulfilling Life—and a Better Career.* New York: Golden Books, 1998.

Rogers, S., and Makonnen, R. *The Entrepreneur's Guide to Finance and Business: Wealth Creation Techniques for Growing a Business.* New York: McGraw-Hill, 2003.

Rusk, T., and Read, R. *I Want to Change but I Don't Know How!* New York: Price, Stern, Sloan, 1986.

Sachs, J. D. *The End of Poverty.* New York: Penguin Books, 2005.

Sadler, W. *The Third Age: Six Principles of Growth and Renewal After Forty.* Cambridge, Mass.: Perseus Books, 2000.

Sedlar, J., and Miners, R. *Don't Retire, Rewire!* Indianapolis: Alpha Books, 2003.

Seligman, M.E.P. *Learned Optimism: How to Change Your Mind and Your Life.* New York: Pocket Books, 1992.

Sheehy, G. *New Passages: Mapping Your Life Across Time.* New York: Random House, 1995.

Sher, B. *I Could Do Anything If I Only Knew What It Was.* New York: Delacorte, 1994.

Stone, M., and Stone, H. *Too Young to Retire: 101 Ways to Start the Rest of Your Life.* New York: Plume, 2004.

Thurow, L. *Fortune Favors the Bold.* New York: HarperBusiness, 2003.

Trafford, A. *My Time: Making the Most of the Rest of Your Life.* New York: Basic Books, 2004.

Tulgan, B. *Managing Generation X.* New York: Norton, 2000.

Ury, W. *Getting Past No.* New York: Bantam Books, 1993.

Vaillant, G. E. *Aging Well.* New York: Little, Brown, 2002.

Vance, M., and Deacon, D. *Think Out of the Box.* Franklin Lakes, N.J.: Career Press, 1995.

Warren, R. *The Purpose-Driven Life: What on Earth Am I Here For?* Grand Rapids, Mich.: Zondervan, 2002.

Weil, A. *Healthy Aging: A Lifelong Guide to Your Physical and Spiritual Well-Being.* New York: Knopf, 2005.

Zander, R. S., and Zander, B. *The Art of Possibility.* Boston: Harvard Business School Press, 2000.

RECOMMENDED ORGANIZATIONS AND WEB SITES

AARP (www.aarp.org)

American Creativity Association (www.amcreativityassoc.org)

American Museum of Natural History Discovery Tours (www.discoverytours. org)

AmeriCorps (www.americorps.gov)

BoardSource (www.ncnb.org)

Boomers!™ Redefining Life After 50!™ (http://p.hostingprod.com/ @boomerstv.com/index.php/)

Center on Aging & Work/Workplace Flexibility at Boston College (http:// agingandwork.bc.edu)

Civic Ventures (www.civicventures.org)

Cross-Cultural Solutions (www.crossculturalsolutions.org)

Doctors Without Borders (www.doctorswithoutborders.org)

Earthwatch Institute (www.earthwatch.org)

Elderhostel (www.elderhostel.org)

Empire State College Center for Distance Learning (www.esc.edu/cdl)

Executive Service Corps Affiliate Network (www.escus.org)

Experience Corps (www.experiencecorps.org)

Global Volunteers (www.globalvolunteers.org)

Habitat for Humanity (www.habitat.org)

Idealist/Action Without Borders (www.idealist.org)

Institute for the Future (www.iftf.org)

International Executive Service Corps (www.iesc.org)

International Senior Lawyers Project (www.islp.org)

Mentor (www.mentoring.org)

MIT AgeLab (http://web.mit.edu/agelab)

National Association of Corporate Directors (www.nacdonline.org)

Osher Lifelong Learning Institutes National Resource Center (www.usm. maine.edu/olli/national/)

Peace Corps (www.peacecorps.gov)
Public Policy Institute of California (www.ppic.org)
SCORE (www.score.org)
Senior Corps (www.seniorcorps.org)
Smithsonian Journeys (www.smithsonianjourneys.org)
University Continuing Education Association (www.ucea.edu)
USA Freedom Corps (www.freedomcorps.gov)
Volunteer Solutions (www.volunteersolutions.org)
World Future Society (www.wfs.org)
WorldTeach (www.worldteach.org)

At the time of this writing, all Web sites were up and active.

Works Cited

Bach, R. *Jonathan Livingston Seagull*. Old Tappan, N.J.: Macmillan, 1970.

Bridges, W. *Transitions: Making Sense of Life's Changes*. Cambridge, Mass.: Da Capo Press 2004.

Buber, M. *The Way of Man*. Wallingford, Penn.: Pendle Hill, 1960.

Buechner, F. *Wishful Thinking: A Theological ABC*. New York: Harper & Row, 1973.

Carroll, L. *Alice's Adventures in Wonderland*. New York: Modern Library, 2002.

Churchill, W. *The Second World War, Volume I: The Gathering Storm*. Boston: Mariner Books, 1986.

Emerson, R. W. *The Journals and Miscellaneous Notebooks of Ralph Waldo Emerson, Volume 5*. Cambridge, Mass.: Harvard University Press, 1965.

Emerson, R. W. *Ralph Waldo Emerson: Essays and Lectures*, Ed. Joel Porte. New York: Library of America, 1983.

Fisher, R., and Ury, W. *Getting to Yes: Negotiating Agreement Without Giving In*. New York: Penguin Books, 1991.

Freedman, M. *Prime Time: How Baby Boomers Will Revolutionize Retirement and Transform America*. New York: Public Affairs, 1999.

Gardner, J. W. *Self-Renewal: The Individual and the Innovative Society*. New York: Norton, 1963 (Reissued 1995).

Garis, H. R. *Uncle Wiggily's Story Book*. New York: Platt & Munk, 1987.

Hock, D. "The Art of Chaordic Leadership." Leader to Leader Institute, available at http://leadertoleader.org/leaderbooks/L2L/winter2000/hock.html.

Honoré, C. *In Praise of Slowness: How a Worldwide Movement Is Challenging the Cult of Speed*. San Francisco: HarperSanFrancisco, 2004.

James, W. *The Varieties of Religious Experience: A Study in Human Nature*. New York: Modern Library, 1994.

Jung, C. G. *The Structure and Dynamics of the Psyche (Collected Works of C. G. Jung, Volume 8)*. Princeton, N.J.: Princeton University Press, 1969.

MetLife Foundation and Civic Ventures. *New Face of Work Survey*. San Francisco: Civic Ventures, 2005.

Potter, C. F. *Technique of Happiness*. New York: Macaulay, 1935.

Seuss, Dr. *Oh, the Places You'll Go!* New York: Random House, 1990.

Thompson, P. *I Don't Feel Old: The Experience of Later Life*. Oxford: Oxford University Press, 1990.

Wolfe, I. S. *The Perfect Labor Storm Fact Book: Why Worker Shortages Won't Go Away*. Atlanta: Creative Communication, 2004.

ACKNOWLEDGMENTS

I thank deeply the colleagues, friends, and family members who helped me create this book and all who shared with me their views on the new perspective replacing retirement. It is also an honor to pass on the ageless wisdom of both portfolio pioneers and New Directions clients and friends, many of whose stories enhance these pages.

I thank especially my assistant, Susan Chiumiento, who always did what needed to be done; transcriber, Pat Jason; and researchers, Claire Burday of New Directions, Chad Remis, and Walter Witte. I thank Barbara Leith, Gregg Wagner, Perry McIntosh, and novelist William Martin for reading or advising me on the manuscript and Ed Parker for his keen eye on illustrations. I thank all New Directions staff who contributed so much, in particular my son, David, who was always there with his calm presence and creative solutions. I thank my daughter-in-law, writer Sarah McAdams Corbett, for pitching in to help research and write many sidebars and two chapters, and writer Abby Russell Prior, for her work on two other chapters.

I thank Rich Higgins, my partner in this project, whose research, editing, and creative writing helped express my ideas and messages with clarity and grace. He's a great collaborator and a believer in portfolios, *not* retirement.

I can only begin to thank Linda, my wife, for her valued help in writing, researching, and proofing. Without her patience, loving support, and encouragement, there would be no book.

D.C.

THE AUTHORS

DAVID CORBETT is the founder and chief executive officer of New Directions, Inc., which helps executives and professionals develop new career and postcareer opportunities in concert with their life goals. A pioneer of the *life portfolio* alternative to retirement, Corbett speaks widely on the topic and has been quoted in publications including the *Wall Street Journal*, the *New York Times, Fortune, CFO Magazine, Kiplinger's*, and many other business publications. Educated at Northwestern University (B.A.) and New York University (M.B.A.), Corbett worked for Johnson & Johnson and spent twelve years in executive search before starting New Directions in 1986. He is an adviser to the AgeLab, an initiative of the Massachusetts Institute of Technology, and a trustee of the U.S.S. Constitution Museum and Andover-Newton Theological School. Corbett and his wife live in Boston.

RICHARD HIGGINS is a writer and editor. His articles or essays have appeared in the *Boston Globe*, the *New York Times, Smithsonian, Atlantic Monthly*, the *Christian Century, Harvard Divinity Bulletin*, and many other publications. He is editor or coeditor of three books, including *Taking Faith Seriously* (Harvard University Press). A reporter for the *Globe* for twenty years, Higgins was recently editor of *More Than Money Magazine*. He has degrees from Holy Cross College, Columbia Journalism School, and Harvard Divinity School. He has three children and lives in Concord, Massachusetts.